WHAT

Every 3rd Grade Teacher Needs to Know

About Setting Up AND Running a Classroom

Mike Anderson

NORTHEAST FOUNDATION FOR CHILDREN, INC.

All net proceeds from the sale of this book support the work of Northeast Foundation for Children, Inc. (NEFC). NEFC, a not-for-profit educational organization, is the developer of the *Responsive Classroom*® approach to teaching, which fosters safe, challenging, and joyful elementary classrooms and schools.

The stories in this book are all based on real events in the classroom. However, to respect the privacy of students, their names and many identifying characteristics have been changed.

ISBN: 978-1-892989-41-3

Library of Congress Control Number: 2010934768

Cover and book design by Helen Merena
Photographs by Alice Proujansky, Jeff Woodward, and Peter Wrenn. All rights reserved.

Thanks to the teachers and students of Foose School, Harrisburg, Pennsylvania; Kensington Avenue Elementary School, Springfield, Massachusetts; King Open School, Cambridge, Massachusetts; Regional Multicultural Magnet School, New London, Connecticut; Sheffield Elementary School, Turners Falls, Massachusetts; Six to Six Magnet School, Bridgeport, Connecticut; Washington School, West Haven, Connecticut; and Wissahickon Charter School, Philadelphia, Pennsylvania, who welcomed Northeast Foundation for Children to take photos in their classrooms.

Northeast Foundation for Children, Inc.
85 Avenue A, Suite 204
P.O. Box 718
Turners Falls, MA 01376-0718

800-360-6332
www.responsiveclassroom.org

Second printing 2012

Printed on recycled paper

CONTENTS

Knowing Third Graders

So you're about to teach third grade? You're in for a treat! As I talk to teachers all over the country, I keep hearing third grade teachers make statements like these:

- "I've been happily teaching third grade for twenty-five years!"

- "I've taught a bunch of different grades, and they're all great, but third grade is my favorite!"

- "It's been seventeen years now, and I still love third grade."

I myself came to third grade after teaching both fourth and fifth grades for several years, and had heard my third grade colleagues make these kinds of statements many times. My mother taught third grade for twenty years and often made similar comments. I remember wondering as I got ready to teach third grade for the first time, "What's the big deal?"

And then the students arrived. Sure, as in any group of children, some held back and some seemed anxious, but by and large, the children who filled the room were notably gregarious and easygoing. As the year went on, I came to see that this enthusiasm and sunny outlook on life mark third grade for most children. Third graders tend to like school, and most are eager to get their hands on their next learning adventure.

My goal in this book is to share some essentials of setting up and running a classroom for third grade students. You'll find information on various aspects of how to manage a third grade classroom, including setting up the furniture, designing effective and fun projects, planning field trips, and developing strong relationships with families. Whether you're brand new to teaching or a veteran teacher who's changing grades, you'll find valuable information that will help make your teaching—and students' learning—joyful and engaging.

1

Know Where Students Are Developmentally

Research tells us, and teachers know from experience, that children change as they grow and develop. Just as children change in their physical characteristics (height, weight, fine and gross motor control, eyesight, etc.), so do they in their other characteristics (attention span, friendship preferences, sense of humor, and willingness to take risks are just a few examples). When we understand the characteristics common to third graders, we can design lessons, create classroom spaces, and group children in ways that will help them capitalize on their strengths.

Common Characteristics of Third Graders

So what stands out among third graders? Of course it's impossible to generalize, but one quality that tends to show up in third grade classes is positive energy. One third grade teacher described it this way: "Third graders are so enthusiastic, and they're willing to try just about anything. 'You want us to sing? Okay! You want us try dancing? Okay! We're going to put on a class play? Cool! Sounds like fun!' It's impossible not to be swept up by their positive energy and enthusiasm."

Interestingly, this same characteristic—unbounded enthusiasm—can also be third graders' greatest challenge. Buoyed by their increasing skills and blessed with seemingly unquenchable energy, third graders are often overly ambitious and tend to bite off more than they can chew. This ambitiousness, coupled with an attention span that often doesn't match their enthusiasm, can lead third graders into taking on big projects that they don't finish or into feeling frustrated and overwhelmed.

Here's a typical third grade scene: A group of students inside for recess on a snowy day decides that they're going to put on a comedy show for the class. With twenty minutes for recess, they feverishly began creating props and costumes for their show without ever actually writing skits or routines. They have just pulled out most of the art supplies for their props when it's time to clean up. "Oooohhh!" they groan. "No fair!" For the next few days, the group keeps work-

Third graders are so enthusiastic, and they're willing to try just about anything.

2

ing at props and costumes (again, without any kind of plan for the show itself) until they get inspired to start a different project, leaving the unfinished props and costumes jumbled in a heap on a shelf.

This sometimes overwhelming enthusiasm is just one characteristic of third graders that it's helpful to know about. There are many others, and some of the most common are outlined on the table on pages 4–6. As you begin to explore the table, here are some important ideas to keep in mind:

■ **Human development is complex.** Even scientists who study it do not fully agree on the means by which humans grow socially, emotionally, linguistically, or cognitively. Most theorists describe the process as a dynamic interaction between a person's biological disposition and many environmental factors—including the historical era in which a person grows up, the person's culture and family, and the institutions he or she encounters (such as schools, places of worship, and the media). The table is not intended to ignore this complexity but rather to offer you a bridge between the abstract ideas of theory and their practical expression in children's classroom behavior.

■ **Every child is unique.** As a result of the complex and dynamic process of development, no two children—not even identical twins with the same genetic make-up—will develop in the same way or at the same rate. Also, a child may develop much faster in one area than in another. For example, a particular third grader might have social-emotional behaviors very common among second graders (such as preferring to work alone or with one friend rather than with a large group) but cognitive behaviors more like those of a fourth grader (such as a greater ability to "read to learn" in content areas).

■ **The table gives you a practical frame of reference.** It lets you prepare for teaching third graders and gives you a resource to check if something puzzling comes up. For instance, once you start teaching third grade, you may notice that many students' handwriting is messy on daily assignments, even though you've seen them do beautiful handwriting when they focus on it. Rather than expending a great deal of energy trying to figure out why they're writing that way or how to "fix it," checking the table and seeing how common this behavior is will allow you to focus your energy on other aspects of writing besides penmanship.

3

■ The table is not about what's "normal." Not all children will neatly fit the descriptions in this table. It's not intended to limit your thinking about students' potential, to support decisions about whether a student is "normal," or to lead you to ignore the needs of students who differ from typical third graders. For example, although many third graders are eager to take on big and ambitious projects, you'll often find some students who approach projects in a different way.

To learn more about child development, see the resources in the "About Child Development" section on page 114.

Third Graders

Common Characteristics	School Implications
Social-Emotional	
■ Enjoy socializing and working in groups.	■ Structure larger-group projects, but expect a mix of socializing and work.
■ Are generally easygoing.	
■ Adjust well to change.	■ Change groupings frequently and use other structures (for instance, whole-group games such as tag and soccer) to stretch children to work across gender lines and with a mix of classmates.
■ Enjoy larger friendship groups, preferably with same-gender friends.	
■ Willing to take risks; usually recover quickly from mistakes or problems.	■ Expect enthusiasm for community-building projects and activities.
■ Concerned with fairness and justice; often have arguments and complaints about fairness issues.	■ Be ready to help with arguments and complaints about fairness and justice.

Third Graders

Common Characteristics	School Implications

Physical

■ Usually full of energy.	■ Give frequent, short movement breaks and incorporate movement into the curriculum throughout the day to boost concentration and productivity.
■ Often hurrying.	
■ May move awkwardly.	
■ Can focus visually on both near and far.	■ Ask for "best" handwriting only on projects and posters, not daily assignments.
■ Tend to play hard and tire quickly.	
■ Have improving hand-eye coordination and fine motor skills.	■ Give time to practice handwriting, drawing, and crafts.
	■ Okay to have children do some copying from the board.

Cognitive

■ Industrious and often overzealous, taking on more than they can handle.	■ Give many short assignments and activities rather than a few long ones.
■ Have limited attention span but can become engrossed in an activity.	■ Break assignments down into manageable parts.
■ Better at using manipulatives to explain their thinking and problem-solving.	■ Give third graders opportunities to sort and organize, but realize they'll often need your help.
■ Usually care about process and product; eager for approval of peers and adults.	■ Display students' in-process work as well as their final products.
■ Increasingly interested in logic, classification, and the way things work.	■ Include study of various cultures—highly enjoyable for third graders.
	■ Craft hands-on math and science lessons that help students grasp abstract concepts.
	■ For read-alouds, offer mysteries and other stories involving logic.
	■ If children become really engaged in a lesson or discussion, go with it if you can; most third graders can comfortably handle a change in plans.

CONTINUED ▶

Third Graders CONTINUED

Common Characteristics	School Implications
Language	
■ Vocabularies are growing quickly; many love to talk and explain ideas.	■ Leverage their love of talking by teaching skills required for conferring in groups, talking with partners, and sharing reflections on their work.
■ Tend to exaggerate.	■ Keep social and academic conferences short, with bite-sized teaching points.
■ Tend to listen well, but have so many ideas that they may not remember what they heard.	■ Invite them to write tall tales and poems using exaggeration, along with nonfiction about what they're learning in social studies and science.

6

The information in this chart is based on *Yardsticks: Children in the Classroom Ages 4–14*, 3rd ed., by Chip Wood (Northeast Foundation for Children, 2007), and is consistent with the following sources:

Child Development Guide by the Center for Development of Human Services, SUNY, Buffalo State College. 2002. WWW.BSC-CDHS.ORG/FOSTERPARENTTRAINING/PDFS/CHILDDEVELGUIDE.PDF

"The Child in the Elementary School" by Frederick C. Howe, *Child Study Journal*, Vol. 23, Issue 4. 1993.

Your Child: Emotional, Behavioral, and Cognitive Development from Birth through Preadolescence by AACAP (American Academy of Child and Adolescent Psychiatry) and David Pruitt, MD. Harper Paperbacks. 2000.

What About Developmentally Younger and Older Third Graders?

Just as every child follows his or her own developmental path, you'll likely find that despite the broad similarities among third grade classes, each class has a somewhat different developmental feel. You'll certainly have children each year who seem or actually are on the young or old side for third graders, and these students may tend to display characteristics common of either second or fourth graders. Here's just a sampling of some of these characteristics, along with a few practical suggestions for how you might adjust your teaching accordingly.

Younger third graders may:

- **Dislike taking risks and making mistakes.** Keep activities low-key and noncompetitive. Younger third graders may be concerned with making their work perfect. Have an ample supply of erasers on hand!

- **Focus eyes on small things up close and struggle to see things far away.** Avoid having students read lots of text or copy lengthy directions from the board.

- **Tend to enjoy smaller work and friendship groups.** When planning cooperative tasks, keep groups small. Be ready to help students meet and greet new students to help expand friendship circles.

- **Want to check in with the teacher frequently.** Allow lots of short check-ins while students are working. Plan for ways students can check in with you throughout lessons and work periods.

If you have developmentally or chronologically older students, they may display many characteristics more commonly seen in fourth grade. The next page provides a few examples and implications for your teaching.

Older third graders may:

■ **Seem overly competitive.** Use activities and language that encourage cooperation over competition. Watch competitive games carefully for excessive competitiveness and criticism of classmates.

■ **Have longer attention spans.** Allow students to run with a great idea—a research project, a fun book project, a movie script—and be there to support and scaffold their work.

■ **Seem overly anxious.** Keep things light and easygoing to help students avoid taking things too seriously. Testing can be especially stressful— avoid heaping on lots of pressure to "do your best."

■ **Push themselves to physical limits.** Offer lots of short breaks and chances to move throughout the day. Balance periods of intense work and play with read-alouds, energizers, and fun games.

How to Use This Book

You might choose to use this book in a couple of ways. For example, you may:

■ **Read cover to cover.** Maybe you're reading this book during the summer before you teach third grade and you have time to read it from beginning to end. Doing that will give you a broad foundation for how to set up and run an effective third grade classroom. You might take notes as you go, or even use your plan book to make specific notes about how to arrange the classroom or set up the schedule at the beginning of the year.

8

■ **Zero in on something specific.** Perhaps you just got your assignment to teach third grade, and the first day of school is a few days away. You don't have much time, and you need to arrange the classroom furniture. Or you may be in the middle of the school year and a particular challenge may have appeared (perhaps around communicating with parents about homework or how to structure a big project effectively). Flip right to the appropriate chapter and skim through until you find what you need. You can always go back and browse the rest of the book when you have more time.

Regardless of how you use this book, consider implementing new ideas slowly. Making too many changes or setting too many goals all at once is likely to end up in failure. Try one or two new things at a time and get comfortable with them before moving on to new changes. Don't worry about making mistakes. The best teachers are also the best learners—ones who try new ideas, make some mistakes, learn from them, and try new ideas again.

Last Word

Third grade is such a fun grade to teach—third graders' enthusiasm is contagious! My son, Ethan, illustrates this perfectly. When he was in second grade, he posted a sign on his bedroom door. Written in large red block letters, it read, "Stay Out!" For those who did make it in, he had posted lists of rules throughout the room about what they could and couldn't do. But at some point as a third grader, things changed. Down came the rules, and he replaced his "Stay Out" sign with a new one: "Welcome!"—written in multi-colored markers with birds and hearts decorating the border.

Is it any wonder that third grade teachers so enjoy teaching?

CHAPTER 1

Classroom Setup

When you take students' common developmental characteristics into account while setting up a classroom, you'll find that they can be much more productive and comfortable throughout the school day. When designing a classroom for third graders, consider a couple of key characteristics: they have tons of energy but easily tire; and they are often gregarious, wanting and needing frequent social interaction. Their need for social interaction means that the traditional seating arrangement I remember from much of my own childhood (with separate desks facing the front of the classroom) would be really tough for third graders to handle. They need to interact with others, talk as they work, and feel like they're part of a group. This is just one way third grade characteristics can affect our classroom setup—read on to learn more.

Arranging the Furniture

There is no one "right" way to organize a third grade classroom. In fact, each year that I taught (regardless of the grade) I created a slightly new room design at the beginning of the year and then usually rearranged everything at some point in the middle of the year. Class size, the academic themes of the room, and even the personalities of students can all be factors in determining how to set up the classroom. Some ideas to consider:

Whole-Group Meeting Area

You'll need to have a place where the whole class can come together in a circle each day for some whole-group work. I begin each day with a *Responsive Classroom®* Morning Meeting in this whole-group circle area. There are also other times to have the whole class gather together. Whether it's to teach

a math lesson, think of solutions to a recess problem, plan a big class project, or simply enjoy a good read-aloud together, a whole-group gathering place will strengthen the class's sense of community and give third graders an opportunity to practice both social and academic skills. The whole-group meeting area is always the first area I set up in a classroom.

As you start to set up a whole-group meeting area, keep these points in mind:

- **A circle is important.** Whether students sit on the floor or in chairs, there should be at least one place in the classroom where they can sit in a circle so that everyone can see and be seen. If space is tight, consider teaching students how to move furniture so there's room to form a circle. (See "I Don't Have Room for a Circle!" on page 14 for more ideas.)

- **Make sure students can sit comfortably.** I find that an area about twelve feet across can comfortably accommodate about twenty third graders in chairs.

Desk Seating

Third graders' gregarious natures and proclivity for talking can be an advantage in some situations and a disadvantage in others, so flexibility is the key to a successful seating arrangement. For example, during group math projects or collaborative science work, it's great for the children to share ideas and excitement—"Whoa! Jimmy! Check out this thing under the microscope!" At other times, however (such as independent reading or testing periods), third graders' tendency to interact with each other can interfere with their learning. At times like these, it can be helpful to separate seating as much as possible. Here are some ideas about striking an appropriate balance:

■ **Spread out.** Having space around them and proximity to just a few classmates helps third graders relax and concentrate. So spread tables out around the room. If you use desks, cluster them in twos and threes. You can put clusters against the walls (if you're pressed for space, try hinging desktops to the walls so you can fold them against the wall when not in use). You can even work a cluster into the classroom library area.

■ **Teach in the circle.** If you teach most of your whole-group lessons from the meeting circle, students don't all need to be able to see a board or screen from their regular work seats. Since moving a lot helps third graders stay fresh and lively, you can teach a lesson in the circle where everyone can see the visuals, have them head back to their seats to work, and then come back to the circle to close the lesson.

■ **Name "regular" seat groups.** I recently visited a third grade classroom that had the name of a continent taped to each desk. Each table group was made up of desks with the names of the same continent (all "Europe" desks together, all "Asia" desks together, and so forth). With this arrangement, regrouping into "regular" seating after furniture had been rearranged for whole-class work was much easier. It also made it easier to direct groups of

When Spreading Out Doesn't Work

If you're not able to create even a temporary circle area, put desks and tables in small clusters in the middle of the room so students will be able to comfortably see you and any visuals you're using during lessons. Be sure to give students lots of movement breaks. For an occasional change of scenery, once you've finished your direct teaching, let students spread out to work on the floor or in any workable space they feel comfortable using.

13

Using Themes to Create Table Groups

Consider using the themes you're studying to create table groups. When studying ancient cultures, the groups could be Incas, Mayas, Greeks, Egyptians, and Chinese. When studying geometry in math, table groups could be parallelograms, triangles, hexagons, pentagons, and octagons.

CONTINUED ON PAGE 16 ▶

"I Don't Have Room for a Circle!"

Unfortunately, this is not an unusual dilemma for teachers. Here are some possible solutions:

1 Create a temporary meeting area.

At meeting time, the children move desks and other furniture to open up a large space for a circle. After the meeting, the students return the furniture to its original place. With adequate teaching and practice, children will be able to do this setup and takedown in just a few minutes.

Three keys to creating a temporary meeting area:

- **Choose carefully.** Choose a spot with as little furniture as possible. Any furniture should be easy for students to move.

- **Use props to define the area.** An easel pad typically works well. Ideally, the easel pad would stay put and serve as the point from which the meeting circle grows.

- **Teach furniture moving.** Use interactive modeling to teach and practice how to move the furniture carefully, cooperatively, and quickly. Try turning the practice into a game, such as beating the clock.

> **Interactive Modeling**
>
> See Chapter 2, "Schedules and Routines," pages 34–37, for a full explanation of interactive modeling.

2 Create it once, use it twice.

Have children move furniture to make room for a circle at the end of the day and gather the class for a "closing circle," in which the children reflect on their day, share about their work, or plan together for the following day. After the meeting, leave the space open—don't move any furniture back. The next morning, the space is ready for a meeting that welcomes the children, affirms the strength of the community, and warms them up for the day ahead. Once the morning meeting is completed, the children move the furniture back. At the end of the day, they repeat the process.

3 Use a space outside the classroom.

Go to the cafeteria, library, gym, or other space in the school that's large enough to accommodate a circle. This solution, admittedly the most challenging, works best when you:

- **Use the same space every day.** The familiarity will help children succeed.

- **Limit distractions.** For example, if you use the cafeteria, meet when no other class is there.

- **Go at the same time every day.** Even if it's not the most ideal time, the predictability will help students feel secure and enable them to focus.

- **Teach the expected behaviors.** Be sure to teach and model transition routines and expectations for behavior outside the classroom.

The whole-group meeting circle is the heart of classroom life. Sitting in a circle, everyone can see and be seen by everyone else. And because the circle has no beginning and no end, it allows everyone an equal place in the group. By the very nature of its design, the meeting circle invites group participation and fosters inclusion. Its presence and prominence in the classroom or in the school day, even if only temporary, says, "In this classroom, we value working together, and we value each individual's contributions to the group."

children: "The 'Asia' table group may now line up for lunch."

■ **Allow changes in scenery.** Third graders will be more productive if they can sit in a variety of places. Bring some beanbag chairs and cushions into the classroom so students can enjoy a quick change of scenery. I remember one third grade student who liked to sit at his desk for math work, in a beanbag chair during reading, and at the counter near the window for writing.

■ **Mix genders whenever possible.** If left to their own devices, third graders will often segregate by gender, but when placed in mixed-gender groups they do quite well.

■ **Mix up friendship groups.** I don't mean that we should separate friends so they can't talk. Far from it—we want to encourage strong friendships in our classrooms. But we can help foster new friendships by occasionally mixing up groups of students so they learn to interact with lots of classmates. Especially once the year is well under way, third graders can really enjoy the challenge and novelty of sitting with new classmates every now and then!

Support Shy or Anxious Students

Not all third graders are gregarious and outgoing, so take care of shy or anxious students. Some may find great comfort in consistency. Consider keeping a good friend nearby when mixing up seating groups. You may even keep a couple of students in the same place if that will be more comfortable for them.

Other Areas of the Classroom

Of course, there's more to the classroom than seats and a whole-group meeting area. Many other areas need to be considered. Few classrooms have too much space, so see the chart on the next two pages for some ideas for designing multipurpose spaces.

However you arrange your classroom furniture in the end, remember that you can always change it later. Third graders tend to be pretty flexible, so they'll be fine (and even excited) if you all spend a Friday afternoon in January moving the furniture around.

Designing Multipurpose Spaces

Area	Tips	Multiple Uses
Circle area	■ Make the area large enough for the whole class to gather in a circle comfortably ■ Include an easel with chart paper for teaching and for recording children's ideas	■ Holding class meetings ■ Teaching whole-class lessons ■ Doing independent work; students can lie on the floor or sit in chairs ■ Doing small-group instruction ■ Enjoying energizers and games
Classroom library	■ Arrange bookshelves with enough space so that several students can browse at once ■ Try a horseshoe shape so that the bookshelves create a cozy space big enough for a worktable	■ Displaying books and storing literacy supplies ■ Doing guided reading or other small-group work ■ Holding one-on-one or small-group conferences ■ Doing other classroom work ■ Doing small-group projects
Theme or content area	■ Have an area for books, displays, and ongoing work for science and social studies units ■ Have a bulletin board or wall display space for rotating charts, posters, and pictures of students working	■ Displaying theme work ■ Working on theme projects or assignments ■ Doing other classroom work

17

CONTINUED

Area	Tips	Multiple Uses
Storage area	■ Have shelves and cupboards for student supplies and materials ■ Keep teacher-only supplies out of sight and out of reach ■ Periodically clean out damaged and worn supplies	■ Storing supplies ■ Hanging coats (place coat hooks on the backs of supply cabinets) ■ Displaying student work (on cabinet doors)
Computer area	■ Keep equipment safely stored when not in use ■ Arrange desktop computers so keyboards can be easily moved	■ Doing research or other computer work ■ Doing regular work when computers aren't in use

Classroom Supplies

Sometimes the difference between good student work and great student work is as simple as the supplies available to students. Having an ample supply of good quality math manipulatives, art supplies, books, and writing equipment can help students more fully engage in their learning. Third graders especially need materials that allow them to do hands-on learning in all subject areas. But third graders can become easily overwhelmed by too many supplies at once. If given the task of making a poster, for example, they're likely to try to use all of the art materials at their disposal.

I remember a third grader who once made a poster for her research project on fish that included buttons, feathers, beads, paints, charcoal pencils, and yarn. It was beautiful and intricate, but she became so set on using every possible art supply that she didn't accurately represent the fish she was trying to describe. Limiting the supplies you provide can be a good way to prevent the frustration that can result from third graders' tendency to bite off more than they can chew.

Three Keys to Keeping Your Classroom Well Supplied

- **Reasonable variety.** Provide a mix of craft supplies, math manipulatives, and art materials so that third graders can find materials to suit their grandiose plans. But rotate supplies throughout the year to keep them feeling fresh while also limiting choices to a manageable number. For example, bring in craft sticks, but remove toothpicks. Bring in watercolor paints while taking away the oil pastels. You can always bring out previously removed supplies later in the year—they'll seem new again!

- **Quality.** As third graders' imaginations explode, they need high-quality supplies that can keep up with their ideas. Scissors that really cut, glue sticks that are clean, and markers that work will all help third graders stay excited and motivated about their work. Consider having students periodically go through supply bins to weed out supplies that are no longer useable. (It's a great indoor recess activity—third graders' developing interest in categorizing and classifying makes tasks like this really fun.)

- **Quantity.** Students need enough of these high-quality supplies to share easily. Some teachers place bins of art supplies in containers at each table group. Others prefer to have larger supply bins for the whole class to share. Either way, make sure you have enough high-quality supplies to go around.

Great Third Grade Supplies

The following chart shows some examples of supplies to have in a third grade classroom, along with quantities for selected supplies. This is meant to be a starting point rather than an exhaustive list. Although the supplies are grouped by category, clearly many materials could fit in multiple categories. Remember that with third grade, not all "early year" supplies should be introduced at once. Some variety is good, but too much at once will overwhelm.

Good Supplies for a Third Grade Classroom

Category	Early in the Year	Later in the Year	Sample Quantities
Art, social studies, projects	■ Crayons ■ Colored pencils ■ Markers (thin and thick) ■ Drawing paper ■ Construction paper ■ Magazines for cutting ■ Yarn ■ Glitter ■ Toothpicks ■ Glue ■ Felt ■ Cotton balls ■ Tape ■ Scissors	■ Hole punch ■ Charcoal pencils ■ Oil pastels ■ Paints ■ Stencils ■ Modeling clay ■ Popsicle sticks ■ Feathers ■ Buttons ■ Seashells ■ Colored tissue paper ■ Wire ■ Wikki sticks ■ Fabric scraps	■ Scissors—one pair for every two students ■ Glue—one bottle or stick for every two students ■ Markers, crayons, colored pencils—an ample supply for each table or desk cluster ■ Feathers, buttons, seashells, etc.—enough for everyone to share; consider allowing students only a limited number of each
Literacy	■ Books, both fiction and nonfiction, multiple genres, both boy and girl main characters ■ Sticky notes ■ Paper for rough and final drafts ■ Pens, pencils ■ Staplers ■ Writing notebooks or journals ■ Clipboards	■ Books (new genres; keep cycling in new books throughout the year) ■ Highlighters ■ Note cards ■ Binders ■ Clear plastic portfolio sleeves	■ Books—a wide range of levels is important to accommodate widely varied reading skills ■ Pens, pencils, etc.—several dozen of each ■ Staplers—two good ones for the class to share

Good Supplies for a Third Grade Classroom

Category	Early in the Year	Later in the Year	Sample Quantities
Math	■ Rulers ■ Base ten blocks ■ Pattern blocks ■ Variety of math games ■ Dice ■ Playing cards ■ Unifix cubes ■ Dominoes	■ Meter sticks ■ Tape measures ■ Calculators ■ Cuisenaire rods ■ New math games ■ Fraction puzzles ■ Graph paper ■ Flash cards and fact triangles	■ Rulers, protractors, calculators, etc.—one for every child ■ Pattern blocks, base ten blocks, Cuisenaire rods, Unifix cubes—a large container for each small group
Science	■ Science journals ■ Bug jars ■ Magnets ■ Plant pots, seeds	■ Magnifying glasses ■ Connex, Legos ■ Scales, balances ■ Critter tanks ■ Other hands-on materials that match your curriculum	■ Enough for partnerships or small groups
Recess (outdoor and indoor)	■ Math/logic games ■ Literacy games—anything that involves word play ■ Joke books (also good for those few minutes when the class is lined up waiting to go to lunch or an assembly) ■ Playground ball, football, basketball	■ Jigsaw puzzles (1,000–2,500 pieces) ■ Mad Libs ■ Quick board games (Mad Gab, Boggle, etc.) ■ Tongue twister books ■ Computer games ■ Snow brick makers ■ Frisbees ■ Jump ropes	■ When supplies are limited (as with playground balls and computers), consider a rotating sign-out system so all students have a chance to use them

See the appendix (pages 105–108) for favorite books, board games, and websites for third graders.

Community Supplies

Consider allowing only "community supplies" in third grade. As third graders become more concerned with fairness, conflicts can arise if some students have a great set of markers (brought from home) but others don't. I've invited parents to do some school shopping for the class at the beginning of the year if they wanted to donate supplies for everyone to share. If students had special materials just for them (or their best friends), I told them that those needed to stay home so that everyone had the same great materials to use at school.

Location of Supplies

When students store materials in their own desks or cubbies, supplies often get lost or broken. Having a system in place for storing supplies so that students all know where they are and how to get them can allow for a neater and cleaner classroom and can help supplies last longer. A few ideas to consider:

■ **Table caddies.** Available at most office supplies stores, table caddies can help organize and store many commonly used supplies (pencils, pens, sticky notes, scissors, rulers, etc.) so that each group of four (or so) has a set of supplies within easy reach.

■ **Shelf storage.** Keep materials such as glue, marker sets, staplers, paper clips, and other commonly used arts and crafts supplies in neatly labeled bins on shelves. Make sure that the shelves are low enough for all students to reach comfortably, or spills and accidents are more likely.

■ **Off-limits supplies.** Some materials such as buttons, feathers, clay, cotton balls, and fabric scraps may come out only for special projects. Some supplies (a digital video camera, for example) may come out only with adult supervision. These kinds of supplies should be behind closed doors or well out of reach. If all supplies are in the same place, third graders (who have a hard time remembering lots of little directions) may be confused about which supplies are okay to use and which aren't.

Classroom Displays

I remember very clearly the first few days before my first year of teaching. I can't tell you how much time I spent trying to cover all of the walls. I had a huge poster of the steps in the writing process. I had a class welcome bulletin board. I had math and literacy reference charts. I had posters and maps. All of that must have been a bit overwhelming for the students as they first entered the room!

I have since shifted from using lots of store-bought and mass-produced posters and displays to primarily displaying work produced by the children themselves. Displaying student work sends an important message: In this classroom, we all share with and learn from one another. Furthermore, students will look at their own work more frequently than at commercial posters.

Tips for building displays:

■ **Build displays slowly.** It's okay to begin the year with some blank walls and bulletin boards. As the class moves through its first units, let the displays track class learning. Children pay more attention to displays that are current and relevant to the work they're doing.

■ **Build displays together.** Ask for student input as to what you should include in your new science bulletin board; have students create some of the words for the word wall; invite students to cut out pictures or make drawings that illustrate what they're learning in social studies. When students play a role in designing displays, they're more interested and invested in them, and the displays are more likely to enhance learning.

Displays of Student Work

Some basics about displaying student work:

■ **Display in-process as well as polished pieces.** This point runs counter to what many of us may believe displayed work should be, but it's important to showcase rough drafts of writing to highlight the revision and editing process. Putting the rough and final drafts of a social studies poster side by side shows that we value the process of learning as much as the product.

■ **Use wall spaces for two-dimensional work.** Display paintings, writing samples, book reviews, and other two-dimensional work on bulletin boards and other wall spaces. Clothespins on draped yarn or pushpins in cork strips are other ways of hanging 2D work on a wall.

Control Clutter!

■ Walls cluttered with charts and papers can appear messy and add to stress levels in the room.

■ Leave ample blank wall space around bulletin boards, anchor charts, and student display spaces. The blank spaces make it easier to focus on individual pieces of work.

■ **Reserve bookshelf tops for three-dimensional work.** Keep the tops of bookshelves clear for dioramas, models, and other 3D pieces.

■ **Consider adding simple shelving.** To create more display space, use simple wire shelving from a hardware store along portions of walls.

■ **Keep displays fresh.** After displays have been up for a couple of weeks, students stop looking at them. When displays reflect current learning, students will find them more interesting.

Informational Displays

Learn More About Classroom Setup at www.responsiveclassroom.org

Classroom Spaces That Work by Marlynn K. Clayton (Northeast Foundation for Children, 2001).

In addition to display spaces for student work, you'll need some spaces for reference charts and other information. Bulletin boards should change continually, right along with the content you're teaching and the time of the school year. Some anchor charts (posters reminding students of lessons or key ideas and facts they should remember) may change often to reflect current learning. Other anchor charts will stay up all year as reminders. Ideally, the boards and charts will be centrally located for easy student reference.

Some good third grade informational displays:

- **Get-to-know-each-other board.** At the beginning of the year, most third graders will proudly share details about their hobbies, pets, families, and favorite school subjects. Create a fun bulletin board highlighting students' lives and they'll eagerly read and learn about each other, making connections that can lead to new friendships.

- **Birthday chart.** Posting everyone's birthdays for easy reference boosts students' sense of belonging in the classroom.

- **Word walls.** Post relevant content-specific vocabulary and commonly misspelled words.

- **Content boards.** Include interesting facts, maps, and pictures for each content area. Place new items on the board slowly (one or two per day) and make a big deal about each new item. Have students help you—many third graders love to organize, arrange, and create displays.

- **Process or format reminders.** Should students sign and date their work in a certain way? Should they use a particular process for turning in homework? Do you have criteria for quality work that you expect all students to meet? If so, create some simple anchor charts and hang them where needed.

- **Routines charts.** Have a sign-up chart for lunch and a sign-out system to use the bathroom. Post by the door an attendance chart that students fill out. Finding ways for children to be independent with these little routines can make for a much smoother day. Without these reminders, third graders—often busy talking to their friends—can lose track of everything they have to do.

- **Writing and reading lesson charts.** Post a chart of key ideas from current lessons.

- **Math lesson charts.** As students practice a new math skill, encourage them to keep checking their work against the chart to make sure they're on the right track.

Technology

Third graders can be quite independent with technology, but they also sometimes know just enough to get themselves in trouble. Left unsupervised, they will often attempt to solve problems on their own, relying on their increasing independence and confidence. I remember a colleague coming into my classroom with a confused look on her face and a handful of Charlie's poetry. "Mr. Anderson, is Charlie having trouble with the printer?" she asked. I turned to see Charlie at the computer with a sheepish look on his face. "Sorry," he apologized. "I kept pressing print because it wasn't working." It turns out that he had reconfigured the printer settings and ended up printing about fifty copies of his poem to a printer at the other end of the school!

While we teach third graders to use the technological tools at their disposal, we must structure and guide their work. A few ideas as you set up technology in your third grade classroom:

- ■ **Monitor students' work.** At times, third graders can be overconfident and unrealistic about their abilities. Just because students say they can work the digital camera doesn't mean they really can. Make sure to directly teach the skills that students need and then monitor closely as they learn to use new technology. Also know your school's policy on what is considered appropriate use of the Internet, teach it to your students, and stay vigilant.

- ■ **Ask for help.** If you're uncomfortable using technological resources, ask for help from a colleague or parent. To ensure that every child can access the technology resources you plan to use, work with the experts in your school on any accessibility issues.

- ■ **Use technology purposefully.** Just because a technology is available or in vogue doesn't mean you have to use it. As with any resource, make sure the technology you use will enhance your efforts to strengthen the classroom community and make learning interactive and child-centered.

Closing Thoughts

Third graders have incredible enthusiasm and energy for learning. Our classroom setup can take advantage of this enthusiasm and transfer it toward deep and meaningful learning, or it can squelch the enthusiasm, leading to frustrated—and frustrating—behaviors and low academic and social engagement. When we pay attention to the common characteristics and needs of third graders as we arrange furniture, design classroom displays, choose materials, and manage other elements of the classroom, we can set up a space that will foster joyful and productive work.

CHAPTER 2

Schedules and Routines

Like all students, third graders benefit from consistency and predictability when it comes to the schedules and routines of the day. However, the energy levels of third graders may be more variable than in other grades—third graders can be bounding with excitement and enthusiasm one moment and laying their heads on their desks in exhaustion ten minutes later. More flexible than their second and fourth grade counterparts, third graders benefit from a teacher who can be consistent yet flexible, able to adjust to students' swiftly changing energy levels.

A story comes to mind. I was observing as a colleague of mine taught a math lesson to a group of third grade students. Andy Dousis was a master at reading the needs of his class, so it didn't escape his attention that some heads were drooping as the after-recess energy dip hit in the early afternoon. Instead of sticking to his plan and forging ahead, he announced, "Okay, everyone! We need some energy. Let's do some yoga. Who's got a suggestion for a story?" Heads and hands popped up around the room. This was a familiar and much-loved activity.

"The Three Little Pigs!" suggested Jillian.

"Okay, everyone up!" Andy called.

"Yes!" responded the students, leaping from their chairs.

The class spent the next seven minutes matching story parts to yoga movements and acting out the story. (You should have seen them howling while using the "downward-dog" yoga position to portray the wolf!) They bounded back to their seats to finish the math lesson with renewed energy. Andy took a few minutes out of the schedule to respond to the students'

29

flagging energy, but the movement break also gave them practice in storytelling. A parent happened to be in the room, and she pulled me aside. "This class is amazing," she whispered. "My son can't sit still for very long, but Mr. Dousis keeps them moving all day. My son just loves school this year. He feels so successful!"

In the following pages, we'll explore how the common developmental characteristics of third graders affect scheduling and see how to construct a schedule that will work well for them. We'll also look at a good method for teaching key classroom routines.

Scheduling

The first step in constructing an appropriate daily schedule for third graders is to think about their developmental characteristics. The next is to list the components of your average day and then order those components by time slots.

Think About Third Graders' Common Characteristics

Energetic and ambitious, third graders are ready to take on the world. They tend to work hard, play hard, and tire quickly. A schedule that respects third graders' needs for intervals of rest and recovery mixed throughout a day of learning will help them be more successful over the course of a long school day.

Some specifics to keep in mind as you think about your schedule:

■ **Stamina.** Especially early in the year, most third graders will have bursts of energy followed by a need to rest and recover. Consider a few short recess breaks instead of one long one (which may tire students to the point where they can't work well afterward). Also try to keep lessons and activities short. Two thirty-

minute math lessons and activities (one in the morning and one in the afternoon) may be more productive than one hour-long math session. Finally, think about alternating active learning periods (such as science explorations) with more quiet and peaceful ones (such as reading).

■ **Social interaction.** Third graders tend to enjoy working and playing with others. When third grade teachers structure collaborative learning and allow some social chit-chat as students work, they help meet this developmental need. Being expected to work alone without talking can be pure torture for third graders and will often result in acting out as students strive to meet their needs for social interaction. Clearly, some periods (for example, reading workshop or testing) require silence, but try to stagger these periods with more socially active ones.

■ **Flexibility.** Third graders tend to be more flexible than students in other grades, so try to go with the flow during the day. If a writing lesson is flagging a bit, stop it early and move on. If students are engrossed in a social studies project, let the period run as long as you can, enjoying the positive energy and enthusiasm. Though third graders can tire easily, I've also seen third grade classes stay focused on independent research projects for more than ninety minutes.

■ **Lesson design.** Third graders benefit from a simple three-part lesson structure:

❖ Several minutes of direct teaching

❖ A longer work period to practice and apply new thinking and skills

❖ A brief wrap-up in which students reflect on and share their learning experiences

When teaching new content, make sure to have enough time for each of these parts.

List the Day's Components

Include both the academic and social components of an average school day. Here's a starting point:

Arrival routine	Read-aloud	Two short recess breaks
Math	Special (music, PE, etc.)	Snack
Reading	Science	End-of-the-day routine
Word study/spelling	Social studies	
Writing	Lunch	

Order the Day

You probably won't be able to create a perfect schedule (if there even is such a thing) since lunch, recess, and specials periods are usually inflexible. Still, you'll arrive at a schedule that optimizes third graders' learning as much as possible if you consider their fluctuating energy levels and their need for movement balanced by periods of rest and recovery.

A couple of ideal schedules are shown on the opposite page for you to adapt as needed.

Two Ideal Schedules

8:30–8:45	Arrival routine
8:45–9:15	Morning meeting
9:15–10:00	Reading workshop
10:00–10:15	Word study, spelling, and snack
10:15–10:30	Whole-class outside game
10:30–11:05	Special
11:05–11:20	Math fact games/activities
11:20–12:00	Writing workshop
12:00–12:20	Recess
12:20–12:40	Lunch
12:40–1:00	Quiet time
1:00–1:50	Math
1:50–2:10	Read-aloud
2:10–2:15	Energizer (movement break)
2:15–3:00	Science and social studies
3:00–3:10	Cleanup and packup
3:10–3:15	Closing circle
3:15	Dismissal

8:30–8:40	Arrival routine
8:40–9:00	Morning meeting
9:00–9:45	Math
9:45–9:50	Math fact games and activities
9:50–10:30	Reading workshop
10:30–10:40	Outside whole-class game
10:40–10:45	Snack
10:45–11:30	Science and social studies
11:30–12:15	Recess and lunch
12:15–12:40	Read-aloud
12:40–1:30	Writing workshop
1:30–1:40	Energizer (movement break)
1:40–2:00	Word study and spelling
2:00–2:15	Catch-up and extensions
2:15–3:00	Special
3:00–3:10	Cleanup and packup
3:10–3:15	Closing circle
3:15	Dismissal

Easing the Recess-to-Classroom Transition

Recess first. Exercising and then eating fits how children's (and adults') bodies naturally work. When physical needs are met, behavior generally improves. If your school schedules lunch first, you may want to suggest trying it the other way around.

Quiet time. Consider having ten to fifteen minutes of silent independent work time when students enter the room after recess and lunch. They can read, draw, catch up on homework, or work on a math or word puzzle. This quiet time helps children shift gears.

Read-aloud. Reading a good book right after recess and lunch can ease any ruffled feelings and help the group settle into the afternoon. See the appendix on pages 105–108 for some favorite third grade read-alouds.

Teaching Classroom Routines

Students don't begin the school year with all the skills they need to function in the classroom, so it's important to intentionally teach routines—even simple ones. Something as seemingly basic as lining up at the door for lunch may need clarification. Is it okay to talk? Should everyone be in a certain order? Do we put supplies away before lining up, or do we clean up after lunch? The more we break down classroom routines and teach each piece carefully, the more orderly and calm the classroom environment will be, freeing the children's time and attention for learning.

Use Interactive Modeling to Teach Routines

Before we get into which skills and classroom routines are most important to teach, let's first look at how to teach these routines to set students up for success. Interactive modeling is a teaching strategy that gives students the opportunity to think about, observe, discuss, and practice the skills needed to perform classroom routines independently. The table on the next page shows what the steps of interactive modeling might look and sound like if you were teaching children how to line up.

Steps of Interactive Modeling: Lining Up Calmly and Safely

Steps to Follow	Might Sound/Look Like
1 Say what you're going to model and why.	"We need to be able to line up in a calm and safe way. Watch while I line up. Be ready to tell me what you noticed."
2 Model the behavior.	Line up calmly and safely. You don't need to narrate as you model.
3 Ask students what they noticed.	"What were some ways I was calm and safe as I lined up?" The children might say, "You walked," "You went right to the door," or "You said, 'Excuse me' when you walked by someone." Name any key behaviors the children miss.
4 Ask student volunteers to model the same behavior.	"Who else would like to show us how to line up calmly and safely?"
5 Ask students what they noticed.	"What were some ways that Lei lined up in a safe and calm way?" The children name specific safe behaviors that Lei demonstrated.
6 Have the class practice.	"Now we're all going to practice lining up at the door. Let's see how well we can do!"
7 Provide feedback.	"Look at that! People were quiet and moved right to the door. I saw some people making room for others as they got into line so that everyone had room. And it took us only thirty seconds to line up!"

Keys to Successful Interactive Modeling

CLEARLY ARTICULATE ROUTINES FOR YOURSELF

Determine what the skill or routine is and exactly how it should look and sound. "Put your backpack away neatly" is not specific enough. Where does the homework that's in the backpack go? Does the backpack always have to go in the same place? Think of possible challenges when children try to follow the routine. For example, what happens in the winter when you might have jackets, boots, and hats to deal with?

Interactive Modeling and Academics

Academic skills and routines (such as using proper punctuation, listening attentively, and passing in homework) can also be taught and practiced through interactive modeling. To learn more, see *Learning through Academic Choice* by Paula Denton (Northeast Foundation for Children, 2005, available at www.responsiveclassroom.org).

KEEP EXPECTATIONS HIGH

Third graders will be more successful with sticking to class routines (even as their heads are filled with exciting new ideas and they're rushing to talk with their friends) once you've modeled and practiced them. If you tell students they need to raise their hands to ask a question, and then three students suddenly call out questions during an exciting math lesson, be firm but matter-of-fact: "Whoops! You need to raise your hand. Then I'll call on you." Once hands are up, call on a student. The class has learned a good lesson: You're serious about the routines you teach, and you have high expectations of the class.

MAKE SURE EXPECTATIONS ARE REALISTIC

We have to be careful, however, about setting standards that are unrealistically high. I remember once when teaching a third grade class, I told students that the expectation was that they would use the bathroom before coming into the classroom after lunch and recess so that no one would have to get up in the middle of writing workshop. It didn't work so well. Students were coming up to me nearly every day and saying, "Mr. A., I really need to use the bathroom!" Many of them told me that they had followed the routine about using the bathroom on the way in, but they had to go again.

I realized that my expectation of no bathroom breaks during the hour after lunch and recess was unrealistic. The children were playing hard at recess,

coming in and guzzling water at the water fountain, drinking even more at lunch, and then getting another sip at the water fountain on their way into the classroom. Of course they were going to need to use the bathroom in a little while! So I created a bathroom sign-out system that enabled students to take care of that need without having to interrupt me. I learned an important lesson: If most of the class seems to be having a hard time following a routine, chances are the problem is with the routine, not the students.

PROVIDE ONGOING REINFORCEMENT AND REMINDING

Interactive modeling is just the first step in teaching routines. Students will need support as they continue to practice. When the class does well, reinforce the positive behavior: "I was just watching you come in from recess, and I noticed that you stopped to let a line of kindergarten students go by. That was following our class rule about being kind to others! Way to go!"

If a routine has been especially tough for a particular student, you might pull that child aside for a private reinforcement when he or she does well: "Mark, I notice you've brought in your homework three days in a row. I know that's something you're working on!" Watch how students are doing and offer quick refreshers when needed: "Our class library is getting a little messy. What are a few things we need to remember about putting books away?" Model the routine again if necessary.

Key Routines to Teach

Although there are dozens of routines to teach throughout the year, a few need to be taught right away—on the first day, if possible. Here are some of the routines I make sure to get in right away when teaching third grade. Remember, it's important to use the structure of interactive modeling when teaching these routines to students. Simply showing them or telling them isn't enough. To be successful, they need guided practice.

Do you have an anxiety dream before each school year starts? Mine is the same every year. I'm standing in the middle of a classroom and students are running all over the place, shouting, throwing things, and jumping off tables. I'm trying to get the group's attention, but no one can hear me. I feel completely helpless and powerless.

We all need a couple of simple signals to get a group's attention. When we model and practice these signals, children respond quite well, enabling us to make smooth transitions and efficiently make a quick announcement.

■ **Visual signal.** Simply raising your hand is a good visual signal. As students see your hand up, they quickly wrap up what they're doing and direct their attention to you. They may also put their hands up to help others see the signal. This signal works especially well when there's a lot of activity and all students can see you.

■ **Auditory signal.** When students can't see you easily or are quietly engrossed in their work (for example, during reading workshop), a chime, pleasant-sounding bell, rain stick, train whistle, or any other pleasing auditory signal can work well.

■ **Student signals for teacher's attention.** Many times during the day, third graders will need to get your attention. Eager and excited students might resort to calling out your name from across the room if they haven't been taught a more respectful signal. Whether it's a hand signal, a thumbs-up, or some other easy-to-use signal, make sure to model and practice it a lot, and then hold students to it.

38

Effective Use of Signals

■ **Keep it simple.** Signals should be easy to use in a variety of settings and easy to respond to. Complex signals, or multiple signals used simultaneously, can be confusing for third graders.

■ **Demand a quick but not immediate response.** Give students fifteen seconds or so to get to a stopping point in their work or conversations before responding. This allows them to better focus on the next set of directions. It's also more respectful. Wait until everyone has responded to the signal before you proceed.

■ **Be consistent.** Students need to know that you will hold them accountable for responding correctly to signals. If your requirement is that everyone stops and looks at you but you let things slide when children don't do this, students won't know for sure how they should respond.

Children need to have snacks to refuel themselves for learning. Third graders do best if they have some downtime to socialize while snacking. So if you can, set aside a few minutes of the morning to take a whole-class snack break (if this isn't possible, choose an appropriate learning activity to combine with snacking).

Tips for Snack Routines

Questions	Possible Solutions
Timing. When's the best time of the morning (or afternoon, depending on your lunch schedule) for snack?	Tacking on snack to the beginning or end of a specials period can work well.
Seating. Will students sit at their seats or can they sit anywhere in the room?	At the beginning of the year, have students sit in a particular spot. Then loosen that up as the year goes forward.
Cleanup. Do students throw away trash and clean tables as they finish, or will you all do that as a class at the end of snack? Will a few people take turns wiping up, or does everyone take care of their own space?	At a class meeting, have the students brainstorm and then choose a method for snack cleanup that they think will work.
Grazing snack. Can students have snacks at other times of the day?	Especially as the year moves on, students may be able to eat some crackers or pretzels as they read a book (make sure to model and practice how that will work).
Community snacks. Will all children have snacks from home? Do children have healthy snacks?	Consider sending a note home to parents asking if they'd be willing to periodically donate snack foods to the class for everyone to share. Make sure to give guidelines for healthy, appropriate snacks.

During the first few days of school, it might make sense to take some regular bathroom breaks as a class—one in the morning and one in the afternoon—to teach the appropriate routines (how to walk down the hall, clean up after yourself in the bathroom, reenter the classroom, and so on). Soon, though, you should work toward having a system in place where students can use the bathroom as needed without having to ask. Some ideas to consider:

■ **Sign-out system.** A clipboard and a pen near the door with a simple sign-out and sign-in chart can work well. If only one student is allowed out of the room at a time, students check the chart to see if it's okay to go. This record might also provide good data if you're wondering whether a student is avoiding work by going to the bathroom frequently.

■ **Bathroom pass.** Some teachers have a simple bathroom pass that students pick up as they leave the room. If the pass is out, students know to wait until it's back. Make sure the pass is small and discreet enough so that it's not embarrassing to carry down the hall.

■ **Proximity.** One year I had a classroom with a bathroom right across the hall. That year, students could just head across to use the bathroom on their own—no sign-out or pass system needed. I could monitor easily from the doorway if needed. Another year, I had a classroom where students needed to travel through other classrooms to use the bathroom. We had to be more structured that year.

■ **Timing.** Are there times when students shouldn't use the bathroom? Unless it's a true emergency, I don't want students using the bathroom during morning meeting, read-aloud times, or reading and writing workshop—all times when disruptions need to be kept to a minimum. I let students know that transitions and active learning periods are better times to use the bathroom.

■ **Model and practice.** Again, we have to make sure to use interactive modeling to teach the routines for using the bathroom. Just telling, or even showing, without giving students the opportunity to interact is of limited usefulness.

RECESS

Third graders tend to be quite cooperative at recess. One year I had a class of third graders who played a complex cooperative game in which wolves chased dogs all over the playground, howling and barking. I never fully grasped the rules of this game, but the students organized it, made up and enforced rules, and helped solve disputes fairly independently for the whole fall. As soon as the ice melted in the spring and the field and playground were open again, the game resumed without a hitch and continued right through the end of the year.

Although cooperative games like "Wolf and Dog" come naturally to many third graders, it's a good idea to play some whole-group outdoor games as a class at the beginning of the year to make sure that students include everyone. As the year goes on, they'll probably do fine on their own, but monitor carefully and be ready to step in with reminders for the group and support for individual children around issues of inclusiveness.

41

Some ideas to consider throughout the year with recess:

■ **Duration.** Remember, third graders tire quickly. A fifteen-minute recess might be enough time to get the blood pumping and recharge their batteries, but half an hour will likely lead to fatigue and a decrease in learning when you're back in the room. A couple of short breaks are better than one long one.

■ **Outliers.** Most likely, there will be children in any class who would like to play but aren't sure how to connect with others. You can help by finding them a buddy who can help them join a game. Letting them take out some recess equipment (for example, Hula hoops or Frisbees) also might help them connect with others. There also may be students who have a hard time playing appropriately with their peers. Organize a group game

for anyone who wants to play so that any child who's struggling will have a way to join other students with an adult's guidance.

■ **Equipment.** How will students bring out (and be responsible for) playground equipment such as basketballs, jump ropes, and kickballs? Consider a rotating sign-out system so students will all have a turn if they'd like. These systems appeal to third graders' developing sense of fairness and help reduce arguments over who gets to bring out equipment. You'll also always know who needs to bring the equipment back in.

■ **Group games.** Consider offering the option of supervised large-group games. One year when I was teaching third grade, I would set up cones on the field on days when I supervised recess. It wasn't uncommon for at least thirty (out of eighty) third graders on the playground to come running over for a game of Blob Tag or Fishy, Fishy, Come Swim in My Ocean.

■ **Signals for lining up.** Make sure to model and practice lining up at the end of recess. Whether you use a whistle, a hand signal, or a loud call ("Line up!"), make a game out of practicing lining up at the beginning of the year. Model it, practice with a stopwatch to see how quickly the class can line up, and then keep trying to break the record. Third graders love these kinds of competitive games!

READ-ALOUD ROUTINES

As I prepared to teach third grade, one of the things that I was most looking forward to was read-aloud time. I was excited to dive into some fun and challenging books like *The Lion, the Witch, and the Wardrobe* by C. S. Lewis and *The BFG* by Roald Dahl. It took only a few weeks of school and a few thousand questions from the students to make me realize

that I was going to need to do some direct teaching about how read-aloud time was going to work in third grade!

Tips for read-aloud time:

- **Set clear expectations.** Make sure students know exactly what you expect of them during read-aloud time. Don't forget to model expected behaviors—as always, just telling the class what your expectations are will not be enough.

- **Choose age-appropriate books.** Third graders are capable of understanding some fairly complex language and themes. On the other hand, just because they can understand complex themes doesn't mean they're ready for them. Third graders can seem quite sophisticated at times, and this can lead adults into letting them experience content that's best left for older children. I recommend finding books with complex storylines and plot twists, but not deeply emotional or adolescent themes. See the appendix on pages 105–108 for great third grade read-alouds.

BEGINNING- AND END-OF-DAY ROUTINES

Many third graders are so busy and eager to move on to the next thing (sometimes without any clear idea of what that next thing might be) that the beginning and end of the day can

Teach Read-Aloud Etiquette

I suggest taking about ten minutes on the first day of read-aloud to teach "read-aloud etiquette." Then post a simple chart of reminders. Here are my requirements for read-aloud time:

- **Make eye contact with me.** Students need to be in a position to make eye contact with me. (They can lie on the floor as long as their heads are up and they're facing me. I sit on the floor and the students surround me in chairs and on the floor.)

- **Pay full attention.** If students want to read along, they may either sit next to me or get another copy of the book. Otherwise, hands need to be free. (This means no hair-braiding, snacking, or drawing.)

- **Raise hands to speak.** When students have questions or comments, they raise their hands. I call on them when I can, but I might need to get to a good stopping place first, so they need to be patient.

My purpose here is to allow everyone to enjoy the story with more attention and fewer interruptions. But there's nothing magical about my three requirements. I know teachers who allow students to eat snacks, color, and so on, during read-alouds. Decide what will work for you. Then deliberately teach the class what's expected so they'll know what to do and you won't have to interrupt reading time to tell them.

43

be quite chaotic times if not carefully structured. As teachers, we sometimes set students up for failure (unintentionally, of course) by giving them too many things to do at once in an unreasonable amount of time. How often do we teach up to the last minute of the day and then tell students that they need to hurry up and pack up homework, stack their chairs, do their afternoon jobs, and get their coats and backpacks on—all as the clock ticks down the seconds to dismissal? And then we get frustrated when students are rushing, running, yelling, and tumbling over each other as they head out the door!

Some tips to consider as you help students have successful and relaxed transitions in and out of the classroom:

■ **Model expectations.** Use interactive modeling to teach students how to begin and end the day. Spend the time practicing at the beginning of the year to set students up for success. This will save you (and your students) hours of frustration later.

■ **Don't give too many tasks.** Give students a manageable number of arrival and dismissal tasks to do: Three is plenty for each of these times. If there is more to do, try to have students do some of them at other times during the day. For example, students might turn in homework on their way to recess or lunch instead of first thing in the morning. Students might also do their daily jobs as an activity before the last teaching period of the day.

■ **Use charts as reminders.** Create anchor charts to help students remember what to do. Hang them in easy-to-see locations.

Anchor Chart Example

When You Enter in the Morning...
■ Hang up coat and backpack.
■ Fill out lunch ticket.
■ Place notes and homework in basket.

Before You Leave in the Afternoon...
■ Pack backpack.
■ Stack your chair.
■ Meet for a closing circle.

DAILY MEETINGS

Consider coming together as a whole class to start the day and to finish it off. A morning meeting (described in the next chapter) is a great way to help third graders transition from home to school in the morning. A "closing circle" can be a calm and focused way to finish a school day. Opening and closing meetings will help ease the transition to and from school and will help students feel safer, more relaxed, and more connected with their classmates and school.

TRANSITIONS

Transitions can be the bane of any teacher's existence if they're not taught and practiced well. A seemingly simple direction such as "Okay, everyone. Put away your snacks, get out your writing notebooks and a pen, and meet in our circle area," can somehow lead to unplanned bathroom breaks, groups of students chatting instead of getting out their work, snack wrappers and yogurt smears left on desks, and a shoving match as students get their writing supplies.

Ending the Day With a Closing Circle

A closing circle can be a calming and focused way to finish a school day. Instead of having students just stand in line as they wait for buses to be called (which may lead to their wrestling on the floor!), consider gathering the class for some quiet reflection or a relaxed game in those last minutes of the day. Here are a few ideas for closing circles:

■ **Partner share.** Everyone chats with a partner for a minute or two about something they enjoyed from the school day.

■ **Around-the-circle share.** Everyone says one thing they learned or practiced during the day.

■ **Favorite game/song.** Does the class have a favorite math or spelling game? How about a favorite relaxing song? These can be fun and calming ways to finish a day.

To learn more, see "Closing Circle" in the February 2011 issue of the *Responsive Classroom Newsletter*, available at WWW.RESPONSIVECLASSROOM.ORG.

45

But when we take the time to set third graders up for successful transitions by modeling expected behaviors, we can actually turn the many daily transitions into nice times—a chance to chat with friends, stretch the legs, and get a change of scenery.

When teaching transitions into and out of the classroom, think about:

■ **Line order.** Consider having the class line up in a designated order to eliminate rushing and shoving to get to a certain spot in line, especially at the beginning of the year. You might have them line up by birthday order or alphabetical order (by first, middle, or last names), or choose names out of a hat. Consider mixing up the methods you use during each day and throughout the week.

- **Routine tasks.** Do students always need to do certain things before entering the room (such as removing coats and hanging them on a coat hook) or before they leave the room (such as cleaning up their work or stacking their chairs)? If so, make sure to practice as a class how these things work.

- **Hallway voices.** What are the expectations for talking in the hallway in your school? For example, perhaps your school has agreed to all use whispers when in the hallway. If so, make sure students know (and practice) what a whisper sounds like. Make sure you follow this rule when talking with colleagues as well so that students know the rule is for everyone, not just children. If your school doesn't have a policy about hallway noise, make sure to talk with students about how you expect their voices to sound in the hall, and then model and practice.

- **Time of day.** Students will naturally struggle with self-control at various times of the day. Perhaps it's the transition coming in from recess. It might be first thing in the morning when twelve buses release students at once. Maybe it's at the end of the day when students are tired and ready to head home. Acknowledge with the class that these might be hard times. Brainstorm ideas as a class about how to help keep these transitions calm and orderly.

When teaching transitions within the classroom, think about:

- **Time guidelines.** As a class, determine how long students should take to transition from one setting to another in the classroom. Try a few transitions and time them to get some initial ideas. Then you can set a timer to help kids stay on track. One teacher I know uses a "cleanup song" whenever the class is picking up from one activity and preparing to move to another. The students literally skip and sing as they clean up and they all have the timing of the song down, so when the song ends, they're ready to move on.

- **Staying relaxed.** When we ourselves are rushed and frantic, our students pick up on that energy and tend to mirror us. When we give students enough time to transition and we stay calm and relaxed ourselves, students are more likely to do the same.

- **Allowing (and even encouraging) chatting.** Third graders tend to need immense amounts of time to socialize and connect with friends. Transitions can be a great time for this to happen. (Consider how you probably like to say "hello" to and connect with colleagues in the hallway as you move from one area of the school to another.) Put the challenge to the class: "Let's see if we can figure out how to talk with each other as we clean up and get ready for our next subject. What are some ideas you have?" Take some suggestions and try them out.

- **Space issues.** If you have a small classroom, a large number of students, or lots of space taken up by furniture or student projects, transitions can be especially tough. Consider transitioning students in small groups to avoid overcrowding (and pushing) in tight spaces. "Anyone who has the long *o* sound in their first name can transition now." "Anyone who has a long *e* sound in their middle name can transition next." Keep going until everyone has been called.

EMERGENCY ROUTINES

Most schools have designated routines that they practice in case of a school-wide emergency. Lockdown drills, fire drills, and tornado drills are just a few. Your students may also have to deal with an in-class emergency at some point (for example, if a student or teacher gets sick), so it's important to practice what to do in these cases. Consider the following ideas and adapt them to fit your particular situation:

- **Students keep working.** If students are working independently, they just keep working.

- **Students read at their seats.** If students are together in the circle or you're in the middle of a lesson, they get out a book and read at their seats.

- **Someone alerts the next-door teacher.** Designate a student to alert the next-door teacher that you've stepped out or you need the teacher to come help you in the classroom.

- **Someone alerts the office.** Designate one or two students to alert the office that you have an emergency.

OTHER ROUTINES

You'll need to teach many routines and social skills each year, and they may vary slightly from year to year, depending on your classroom and your students' needs. Again, use interactive modeling to directly teach and practice the routines students need to know. Here are some possibilities:

- Indoor recess routines

- Taking care of supplies in the classroom

- Greeting classroom visitors in a friendly way

- Caring for class plants and pets

- Asking someone to join a game

- Walking in the hallways

- Behaving appropriately at assembly

- Signing out playground equipment

Closing Thoughts

Third graders are so eager to dive right into work and projects that it can be tempting for us to skip the direct teaching of routines and procedures or to just briefly outline what needs to happen. We're counting on students' enthusiasm and energy to carry the day. However, when we neglect the careful practice of the daily routines that enable students to function effectively, we'll often spend inordinate amounts of time later in the year trying to hunt down student work, cleaning up messy tables, and settling scuffles at supply areas. The time we invest in directly teaching students how to navigate the classroom effectively is well worth it and will pay dividends throughout the year.

CHAPTER 3

Building Community

In the summer, before the students arrive, it can be easy to focus on just about everything *except* the students. In early August, we start to play with the furniture, moving desks and tables around and trying to work in a bookcase we just picked up for five dollars at a yard sale. As August draws on, we focus more and more on getting the first academic units of the year ready to go. We organize math supplies. We sift and sort through books to include in our class libraries. Schedules are also finalized in the last week or two before school starts. We figure out when we have art, music, PE, computer class, and library. Special education and remedial teachers appear at our door letting us know that they need to see several students several times a week. We have so many things to plan for as the start of school approaches!

And then the students arrive. And they're little people. With personalities. They have likes and dislikes, interests and aversions, friends, and social histories. Perhaps one of our biggest jobs at the beginning of each school year is bringing this eclectic and sometimes challenging mix of students together and cultivating a cohesive, cooperative, and vibrant classroom community.

There's no doubt that this is easier in some years and harder in others. Some years, students enter the room relaxed and easygoing with solid sets of friends who treat others kindly. But just a couple of students with challenging behaviors or a few students who haven't worked well together in the past can create some tense social dynamics. What's important to recognize, however, is that as teachers, we can help third graders come together and gel as a unit. This chapter will offer many ideas to help build a strong community as you begin the year with a new third grade class.

51

Getting to Know One Another

One of the most important things we can do at the beginning of a school year is to help students get to know one another. This class will need to work together in a variety of capacities throughout the school year, and to do that effectively, children will need to know each other well.

Learning One Another's Names

It always astonishes me when children reach third grade and still don't know all their classmates' names. But it happens. Here are some ways to help students learn each other's names at the beginning of the year:

■ **Post names around the room.** Wherever you can, get students' names up on walls and other surfaces. Label students' cubbies, desks, and coat hooks. Create posters with bus groups, line orders, and lunch sign-up charts. These will help students learn each other's names more quickly and gain a greater sense of ownership of their classroom.

■ **Wear name tags.** For the first week or two of the school year, have students wear name tags. Make sure everyone wears them so that students can use one another's names throughout the day. Later in the year, these name tags can be kept in a bin on a shelf so that when you're out for the day, or you have a guest presenter coming in, or a new student joins the classroom, students can quickly put their name tags back on again.

■ **Play name games.** When lining up for lunch, or sending table groups to the circle area, or transitioning from a read-aloud back to desks, play games with students' names: "If you have an 'H' in your last name, you may line up." "Students who have at least two different vowels in their first names may line up." "If you have more than six letters in your middle name, you may line up." These kinds of simple, playful name games keep the tone upbeat and help students think about each other's names as they move about their day.

The Importance of Positive Teacher Language

Classroom community begins with the teacher. Our tone and demeanor influence students' mood and tone, which in turn influence their ability to form meaningful bonds with one another. To learn more, see *The Power of Our Words: Teacher Language That Helps Children Learn* by Paula Denton, EdD (Northeast Foundation for Children, 2007), available at WWW.RESPONSIVECLASSROOM.ORG.

Greetings

It's amazing how powerful a simple greeting can be. If I walk into my school and a colleague acknowledges me with a quick and sincere "Good morning, Mike!" I immediately get a quick boost of energy. It feels good to be recognized. It's important to feel welcome. Having students greet each other can be a great way to start the day, helping everyone feel like an important member of the classroom community.

For years now, I have used the *Responsive Classroom®* structure of Morning Meeting, and a greeting is the first component of that meeting. Students join together with me, sitting in a circle to begin each day. At the beginning of the year, greetings are simple and straightforward. We might take turns around the circle saying "Good morning" to each other, practicing using each other's names with a friendly voice and smile. As the year progresses, we add other important elements such as shaking hands. Further on in the year, we'll learn more complex and playful greetings that might include high fives, pinky shakes, or the ever-popular fist bump.

Even if you don't use the full *Responsive Classroom* Morning Meeting structure, a greeting can be a powerful way to begin the day. Here are some tips for effective greetings:

■ **Set the tone.** Set a respectful and sincere tone for greetings right from the start. This shows that greetings are an important part of the day and something everyone should take seriously.

■ **Start simple.** Begin the year with a simple, low-risk greeting in which each child turns to the next child in the circle and says, "Good morning, _____." Gradually introduce more complex greetings.

■ **Always model.** Use interactive modeling for all new greetings so that students know how each greeting should look and sound (see Chapter 2, "Schedules and Routines," pages 34–37, for more on interactive modeling).

Interactive Modeling of Greetings

Steps to Follow	Might Sound and Look Like
1 Say what you're going to model and why.	"One of our rules is to 'Treat everyone with respect.' Each of you will greet someone in a respectful way today. I'm going to greet Jorge. Watch what I do."
2 Model the behavior.	"Good morning, Jorge." (Use a friendly tone and show a friendly smile.)
3 Ask students what they noticed.	"What did you notice about how I greeted Jorge?" (If necessary, follow up with questions such as "What kind of voice did I use?" or "What did you notice about my face?" to prompt children to list the important elements: friendly voice, friendly face, used his name, etc.)
4 Ask student volunteers to model the same behavior.	"Let's have two people volunteer to greet each other in those ways."
5 Ask students what they noticed.	"What did Bridgette and Micah do as they greeted each other?"
6 Have the class practice.	"Now we're all going to practice. I'm going to partner you up, and you're going to try greeting your partner. Let's see how well we can do!"
7 Provide feedback.	"I saw lots of people using friendly faces and voices. It sounded like many people remembered to greet their partner by name. That was a great start!"

54

Learn More About Greetings and Morning Meeting at www.responsiveclassroom.org

The Morning Meeting Book by Roxann Kriete (Northeast Foundation for Children, 2002).

99 Activities and Greetings: Great for Morning Meeting . . . and other meetings, too! by Melissa Correa-Connolly (Northeast Foundation for Children, 2004).

Morning Meeting Greetings in a Responsive Classroom DVD (Northeast Foundation for Children, 2008).

■ **Emphasize inclusiveness.** Third graders will tend to sit with and greet the same people again and again, so we need to help them feel comfortable greeting everyone. Make sure to mix things up so that everyone greets lots of different people. Third graders love a challenge, so try something like this: "Today, your challenge is to greet three people you don't often play with at recess!"

■ **Guide when necessary.** If students continue struggling with inclusiveness, be more direct. Assign seats and do an around-the-circle greeting. Or you might have students pick names out of a hat. You could even go back to a more basic greeting, where students simply greet the classmate next to them.

Good Greetings

For the Beginning of the Year

■ Turn and say, "Good morning, _____."

■ Pass an object (such as a pencil) around the circle while saying "Good morning, _____."

■ Pass a handshake and "Good morning, _____" around the circle.

■ Greet and shake hands with the person on your right and on your left.

For Later in the Year

■ Greet using each other's last name: "Good morning, Mr. _____."

■ Try a category greeting: "Greet someone who likes art" or "Greet someone who walks to school."

■ Skip count around the circle: "Greet every third person."

■ Greet someone in a different language: "Hola, Charlie!" "Bonjour, Jill!"

■ Greet someone and ask a question: "Good morning, Ani. What's your favorite animal?"

Getting-to-Know-You Activities

Another great way to come together at the beginning of the year is to structure some getting-to-know-you activities. Some of these activities that are particularly well-suited to third grade are shown on page 56.

Sample Getting-to-Know-You Activities

Activity	Instructions	Tips	Academic Connections
Student graphs	Students choose something they'd like to know about their classmates (such as their favorite foods or animals). Students then create multiple-choice surveys for everyone to fill out, compile the data, and create a colorful bar graph to display in the room.	Show students a sample survey before having them create their own.	Collecting data, tallying, graph making, answering multiple-choice questions.
Student interviews	Partner up students who don't know each other well. Have students write interview questions and interview their partners. Next, give students pictures of their partners mounted on a large sheet of paper. Students can then create a fun art display that will teach others about their partners.	First conduct a whole-class brainstorming session on interesting questions to ask each other.	These interviews can also allow you to collect rich data about students' abilities in areas such as fine motor skills, interpersonal skills, handwriting, spelling, and creativity.
Group challenge	Group students into teams of four or so. Challenge them to find, within a time limit, as many things group members have in common as possible. For example, they might find that all group members were born in different states, have a sister, and love spaghetti. Groups record their commonalities and share them with the whole class. Do this activity every day for a week, each time shuffling students into new groups.	As a class, brainstorm ahead of time to come up with categories of possible commonalities to investigate.	Categorization and sorting.

You'll likely come up with many more ideas. Keep in mind that good getting-to-know-you activities are ones that:

■ Everyone can do successfully

■ Are fun and engaging

■ Help children make personal connections with one another

■ Show students that this class cares about who they are

■ Allow you to assess students' social and academic abilities

Sharing

Another component of *Responsive Classroom* Morning Meetings is sharing. Whether or not you lead your class in this particular type of sharing, setting aside a bit of time each day for students to share personal information with one another can help set a collaborative and empathic tone in the classroom. When students share about themselves, they also gain valuable practice in a variety of academic and social skills. Making eye contact with an audience, using a clear voice, being succinct, and responding to questions and comments are just a few of these skills. Possible formats for sharing:

■ **A few people share each day.** Set aside several minutes each day for a few students to share something that's simple and interesting from their lives: having a birthday dinner at a grandparent's home, getting a puppy, reaching a new level in a video game, and so on. Model for students how to share one main idea with a couple of supporting details. Also model how listeners can ask sharers good questions.

■ **Around-the-circle sharing.** Friday afternoon is a good time to learn and practice around-the-circle sharing: "What's one thing you enjoyed doing in school this week?" "What's something you're looking forward to this weekend?" Each student shares one sentence. Around-the-circle sharing can also be used before and after vacations, when lots of students want to share, and at the beginning or end of academic lessons to help students reflect: "What's something you're going to practice as you write your poems today?" "What's something that was hard for you about the geometry puzzles we were trying?"

■ **Partner sharing.** Having short and meaningful conversations with classmates is a skill that students can use throughout the day. Students can begin practicing this skill with social topics ("Share with someone next to you what kind of animal you would be if you could change for a day"). Later, they can practice this skill using academic topics ("Share with a partner one thing you learned today").

No matter what format you use for sharing, remember to use interactive modeling to give students a chance to practice the skill.

Keeping Sharing Safe for Everyone

Sometimes students choose to share topics that aren't appropriate for the class to hear. Or a student wanting more attention may make up elaborate stories that leave classmates confused or annoyed. The following suggestions will help you set up sharings that are appropriate and successful.

■ **Brainstorm appropriate topics.** Before students start sharing, have the class brainstorm a list of suitable topics: pets, friends, trips, hobbies, family events, and so on. Hang this list in the circle area for easy reference.

■ **Model only appropriate topics.** As you model sharing, make sure the topics are simple and interesting. Make them the stuff of everyday life, so students see that they don't need to impress people with really exciting stories.

■ **Preview sharings.** At the beginning of the year when you're still getting to know the students, have them quietly tell you what they want to share ahead of time to make sure it's appropriate. This can be a great way to coach children on how to share while also checking to make sure the content is appropriate.

■ **Set the expectation that sharings will be appropriate.** Say something like this to the class: "If you think anyone would be embarrassed or upset by something that you're thinking of sharing, tell it to me privately first to see if it's okay to share."

■ **Be ready to cut off inappropriate sharings.** When a sharing is sounding inappropriate, quickly but respectfully cut the student off. For example: Thomas says, "Last night my uncle came over and he'd been drinking a lot . . ." and you interject, "Thomas . . . hold on. I'd like to check in with you later about that sharing to make sure it's okay for the class. Let's move on to Juanita's sharing for now."

For more information about sharing, see *The Morning Meeting Book* by Roxann Kriete (Northeast Foundation for Children, 2002) at www.responsiveclassroom.org.

Class Events and Projects

Since many third graders love working with others and are excited about taking on big projects, collaborative work is a fantastic way to build community. Here are some ideas for great third grade projects:

■ **Field trip.** Consider taking a simple field trip near the beginning of the year, perhaps even just walking to a local business or park. A field trip can provide shared experiences that everyone can savor and remember and can offer a great foundation for future collaborative ventures.

■ **Class pet.** Andy Dousis, a long-time third grade teacher, often had students decide upon a class pet. After researching costs and care, the class had to choose a name, figure out a routine for cleaning the cage, and talk about how to feed and handle the pet. All this provided opportunities for the class to learn to make important decisions together. (Find out your school's policy on having class pets before you bring the topic up with the children.)

■ **Class singing.** Susan Trask, who taught third grade for twenty years, told me about one of her greatest joys: Wednesday morning sings. After just a few forty-five-minute sessions, the class had a shared repertoire of favorite songs, which grew as the year went on. Some of the songs were just good old-fashioned fun (such as "Row, Row, Row Your Boat" sung in a round) and some reinforced academic content around themes (such as civil rights and Native American studies). The important part for her, though, was the sense of community that arose while singing.

■ **And many more.** Other ideas that third grade teachers may want to consider to help a class pull together around a common goal include running a school store, holding a class tag sale, visiting a local nursing home, starting a class garden, and buddy-reading with kindergartners.

Recess

For naturally gregarious and social third graders, recess can be a favorite time of day. Often able to navigate and hold on to complicated rules and social structures, third graders generally thrive during this less-structured time of day. Nonetheless, like all children, they need adult guidance to keep recess conflicts to a minimum. Here are some ideas for making recess safe and fun for *all* third graders:

Teach Recess Behaviors

Even if you don't have recess duty, be sure to teach students expected recess behaviors, just as you teach expected classroom behaviors. Interactive modeling (explained in Chapter 2 on pages 34–37) is a great technique for helping students learn how to negotiate the many challenges of the playground. Key recess behaviors to model are:

■ How to use structures (swings, slides, etc.)

■ Where to get and put away equipment (balls, Hula hoops, and so on)

■ How to get an adult's attention

- What to do if someone is hurt

- How to stay within the play area

- How to respond to the signal for lining up

- How to come back into the building

- Where to put lunch bags

- How to include everyone who wants to join a game

- How to ask to join a game

- How to choose sides

- How to be a good sport whether your team is winning or losing

Offer Structured Choices

One year when I taught third grade, two teachers shared recess duty, supervising about eighty children. Each day, one of us would take care of general supervision, walking through the playground, chatting with students, and watching to see how things were going. The other would set up cones on the field and play some kind of tag or other running game with students who wanted to join. It was a rare day when fewer than ten students joined, and some days we had as many as thirty. For students who struggle with joining a game on their own or playing fairly with others, a supervised game or activity can be a great source of security and fun.

Great Third Grade Recess Games

Blob Tag. A student starts as "it." When the student tags someone, the two join hands and run together as a blob. When they tag someone else, a trio forms. Once a fourth person is tagged, they can stay together or split into two separate blobs. Blobs can split apart and rejoin throughout the game as long as everyone who has been tagged is holding hands with at least one other person. The game ends when everyone has been tagged.

Alaskan Kickball. Each person gets one turn kicking per inning. Once students kick the ball, they run around teammates, who are lined up down the third base line (other bases are not used). The team gets a run for every time a runner gets around all the teammates before the fielding team gets the ball back to home plate. Once everyone has had a turn to kick, the teams switch.

Obstacle courses. Bring out a stopwatch and make up obstacle courses around the playground. (Touch the slide, crawl under a swing, do five jumping jacks, and run around the basketball court.) Third graders love to race the clock!

Keeping Tag Games Safe for Everyone

Teach safe tagging. Use interactive modeling to teach and practice how to tag with one open hand on the shoulder. Teach how to avoid the "bathing suit zones." (Any body area that's normally covered by a bathing suit is off limits when tagging.)

Start off slowly. The first tag games can be simple ones (even walking ones) where the goal is to practice safe tagging. As the class is ready, introduce more complex and energetic tag games.

Monitor carefully. Hold students to high behavior expectations. Reinforce safe tagging: "Wow! You were all taking care of each other with safe tagging. You used gentle touches and tagged each other on the back or the shoulder." Redirect unsafe tagging: "Toni, use an open hand when tagging. You can try again in the next round."

Teach Games to Your Class

At a time other than the whole-grade recess, teach the class some recess games. In addition to helping your class build community, you're helping to spread appropriate and fun games to the rest of the grade level, because these students will teach other friends at the whole-grade recess. (See the boxes on pages 61 and 63 for game ideas and resources.)

Supervise

When you see small misbehaviors, speak to the students immediately and redirect their behavior. Nipping small things in the bud is essential to reducing behavior problems and keeping recess running smoothly. For example, if you see a child take the ball away from a student who is pitching in kickball, intervene, even if the other student doesn't put up a fight.

62

Play With Students

Even if you're not structuring a large game for the grade, you can still join in and play basketball, hopscotch, or jump rope. You can then set a good example for how to follow rules, lose and win gracefully, and treat others kindly while playing. It's also lots of fun for students when their teachers join in!

Lunchtime

Lunchtime should be a pleasant and relaxing time when third graders get to eat, socialize, and recharge their batteries for an afternoon of learning. Without adult guidance, however, lunchtime can become a source of anxiety, frustration, and isolation for students.

As with all other behaviors we want students to adopt, we need to explicitly teach students lunchtime behaviors. The more we do this, the more successful students can be. We can also help students by setting up structures that make lunchtime more enjoyable.

Modeling in the Cafeteria

Whether or not you have lunch duty, you can still help set students up for success in the cafeteria. Use interactive modeling to teach students the procedures and routines they need to know. It's best if you do this teaching in the cafeteria itself. If you can't do that, you can teach lunchtime behaviors in the classroom. If the lunch monitors (or other lunch monitors if you're one of them) can be with you and help with the modeling, so

---

You Don't Have to Do Recess Alone!

Don't have much game experience? Wondering how to play with and watch thirty children outside? Look to these resources for help:

- **Colleagues.** A colleague can go to recess with you and teach games to your class while you participate. Or the two of you can divide up the group. One year, I played group games with interested students while a colleague monitored the rest of the playground.

- **Parents.** Invite a parent to teach recess games while you set the tone, manage the class, observe, and participate.

- **Books.** Two great outdoor games books are *36 Games Kids Love to Play* by Adrian Harrison (Northeast Foundation for Children, 2002), at www.responsiveclassroom.org, and *The Ultimate Playground & Recess Book* by Guy Bailey (Educators Press, 2000).

much the better—that will ensure that everyone is on the same page with lunchtime routines and expectations.

Other Ideas for Successful Lunchtimes

In addition to modeling routines and behaviors, we can also do the following to help set third graders up for success with lunch:

Key Cafeteria Procedures to Model

- Lining up for food
- Paying or using a ticket system
- Finding a seat
- Responding to the signal for attention
- Using the bathroom
- Throwing away trash
- Lining up for dismissal
- Cleaning tables and floors
- Using an appropriate voice level

■ **Assign lunch buddies.** Especially at the beginning of the year, it can be comforting for third graders to know the classmates they're going to eat with before they head to lunch (just as teachers tend to plan who they're going to eat with at a professional development conference). Assigning lunch buddies or table groups can be a great way to start the year.

■ **Consider music and décor.** What are some things that make eating out at a nice restaurant enjoyable (beyond not having to cook or clean up)? Soft music in the background, relaxed lighting, comfortable chairs, flowers on the table.... How does your school cafeteria compare? Now, I'm not advocating that school cafeterias be five-star dining experiences, but there are things we can do to make cafeterias more pleasant. Consider talking to your school leaders about putting some plants on the tables, putting up some wall hangings, dimming the lights if possible, and playing some pleasant music. It's amazing what these manageable changes can do for the atmosphere of a cafeteria.

■ **Brainstorm conversation topics.** Having the class come up with interesting and appropriate topics for lunchtime conversation can ease anxiety between partners who might not otherwise know what to talk about.

■ **Plan for the last five minutes.** Most trouble in the cafeteria happens in the last five to ten minutes when students have finished eating and are looking for entertainment. Having baskets of things to do at each table can help occupy children who finish early. Simple items might include playing cards, Mad Libs, crayons and paper, and word searches.

Maintaining a Strong Community

When I wrote the first part of this chapter, I mostly had in mind the beginning of the school year, since the first six weeks of school is a critical period for helping students get to know each other and build a sense of community as a class. But how do you maintain that sense of community over time? Community-building work might be most intense and deliberate at the beginning of the year, but if our class community is going to stay strong, we need to keep nurturing it all year long.

Recognize a Class's Identity

Each class of students is different. One year, a class may love to play group games outside. Another year, there's a strong inclination toward arts and crafts. The next year, a few history buffs spread enthusiasm for learning about American history. As the year progresses, pay attention to whether positive group identities emerge and then nurture them. For example, for the class that has multiple history buffs, bring in a bin of history books for students to check out. For the class that loves arts and crafts, introduce some new supplies and talk about ideas for using them during indoor recess.

As we start to describe a class as having many "historians," "artists," "music lovers," or any other positive designation, the class will begin to feel a sense of group pride and positive connection with classmates. I do, however, want to offer a couple of cautions.

First, we're looking for a sense of class pride and identity, not a sense of superiority. Avoid making comments that compare classes, such as "We've got the best class in the third grade because…" or "You guys are so awesome! You're the best artists in the school!" These kinds of statements can lead to competitiveness among classes.

Another caution is to avoid labeling a class with negative attributes—a class that's "irresponsible" about getting its homework in on time or "disrespectful" toward substitute teachers. Though it's important to address problems like these if they arise, we should do so without labeling the class. This way we remain respectful ourselves, and we avoid the dangers of the self-fulfilling prophecy!

Build Community Through Learning

Third grade offers countless opportunities to build and maintain class community through academic activities. Consider some of the following ideas:

Maintaining Class Community Through Academics	
Idea	**Examples**
Daily sharing	■ At the end of a reading period, students can share a text-to-self connection they made with a character in the book they were reading. ■ In the middle of a math class, students could turn and talk with a buddy about one thing they think they understand well. ■ During writing, students can request a peer conference to have a peer help them with editing or revising. ■ At the end of a science lesson, students can share around the circle one question that came up for them as they worked on their experiments or projects.
Unit celebrations	■ Invite parents to an informal open house to see social studies projects. ■ Have the class create a bulletin board in the hallway to showcase favorite poems with illustrations. ■ A class that has grown flowers as part of a plants unit can arrange to have the flowers put in the cafeteria or delivered to a local hospital.
Class website (make sure to follow your school's or district's policy about Internet use)	■ Once a week, students update the class website by sharing what they learned that week.

A Strong Finish

As I write this, it's late May and I'm seeing the effects of the end of the school year in children. Their emotions are all over the place. Highs are really high, and lows are *really* low. I get it. The end of the school year is an emotional time. Many students are eager for summer vacation. Some inwardly dread the unstructured time away from school. As the weather warms up, attention to schoolwork tends to fade. And perhaps most difficult for teachers who have worked so hard on building a strong sense of belonging, the classroom community can feel as if it's falling apart.

I've heard some teachers argue that it's best to mention the end of the school year as little as possible, because the more we talk about it, the more students will stress out about it. In my experience, the reverse is true. Come April, students are already stressing out about it, so I think it's important to spend time and energy talking about the transition to fourth grade and refocusing students on their classroom community. As in every other aspect of classroom life, the more we set children up for success, the better.

End-of-the-Year Meetings

As the year winds down, hold frequent group meetings to discuss the transition from third to fourth grade. Have students share their questions and their concerns. "When will we know who we have for a fourth grade teacher?" "Who will be in my class?" "Can I come back and visit you next year?" These are just a few of the questions that will surface. Consider letting everyone write down questions on note paper and putting them in a question box. During each meeting, you could answer a couple of them.

Culminating Project

A culminating project can be a great way to keep the sense of community strong through the end of the school year. One year, a class wanted to make a movie. I had just read *A Wrinkle in Time* by Madeleine L'Engle as a read-aloud, so we rewrote the book into a screenplay and small groups of students came into school an hour early for about three weeks while we taped the movie around our school.

Some other fun ideas for an end-of-the-year project:

- **Class Jeopardy game.** Students create questions from their learning and shared experiences throughout the year. Categories might be weather, geometry, read-alouds, and funny events. Play the game as an afternoon event during your last week (make sure to deemphasize the scoring and keep it relaxed).

- **Fruit salad social.** This is a healthy alternative to an ice cream social. Have the class brainstorm fresh fruits and toppings that might work well. Then the class can prepare the feast and enjoy. This would be a fun event to do in the evening so that families could join in.

- **Class movie night.** Students can wear PJs, eat popcorn, and sprawl on the floor while enjoying a movie together. If you're really brave, turn it into a sleepover—have a few parents stay to chaperone with you, and clear your Saturday to catch up on sleep.

- **Time capsule.** Have students create and store mementos from the year in a box. Decorate the box and show students where it will be kept. Let them know they'll get to come back together at the end of next year (or another year) to open the box together.

- **Sharings with incoming third graders.** Come up with some projects and fun events that will allow students to share some of the great things they did in third grade with the incoming third graders. This will give the class a great sense of accomplishment.

Connect With Fourth Grade

The more we can demystify the coming year for students, the more relaxed they'll be as they finish third grade. Here are just a few ways to help third graders know more about what to expect in fourth grade:

- ■ **Meet the teachers.** Bring the third grade class to meet the fourth grade teachers. Or have those teachers come visit your classroom.

- ■ **Invite fourth graders to a Q&A.** Have fourth graders come in and run a Q&A session with the class to give students a child's-eye view of fourth grade.

- ■ **Look ahead.** Share the major units taught in fourth grade. Let students talk with each other about what they know about those units and what they're looking forward to learning.

- ■ **Take a visit.** Find time to visit the fourth grade classrooms so students can get a feel for what they're like.

- ■ **Learn who's in next year's class.** If your school doesn't place students in their classes until the summer, you can advocate for having the placement process finish before the school year ends so that students can find out who'll be in their classes. Knowing this well in advance can be enormously comforting to third graders heading into fourth grade.

Closing Thoughts

Some teachers may argue that although building community is nice, we simply don't have time to do it because we need to focus on academics and prepare students for testing. And although it's true that we do have to focus on academics, and testing is a reality of public schools right now, I contend that to really focus on academics it is vitally important to spend time building a strong community of learners. When children feel safe and valued in their class, when they know they can take a risk, and when they feel a sense of positive community membership, then they're able to more fully engage and be successful in the important academic work of third grade.

Classroom Games, Special Projects, and Field Trips

My son, Ethan, is starting third grade. Here's my hope: As he steps off the bus at the end of a long day of school, he can't wait to tell me about all of the fun projects he's been working on. I imagine him saying, "Dad! We're doing this awesome ecology study in school right now! We're going out and catching bugs and letting them go in this huge tank. Then we take turns observing and recording notes. I got to see a praying mantis eat a bumble bee today! Can we go out so I can catch some more stuff for the class tank? Please?"

As teachers, isn't that the way we want school to be? We want students to be fired up and enthusiastic, engaged and motivated. Even though all of every school day can't be filled with hands-on, experiential learning, we can breathe life into the curriculum and classroom through the regular use of games, special projects, and field trips.

While you're thinking about games, projects, and trips for your class, it's helpful to remember how common characteristics of third graders might affect your plans. Some things to keep in mind:

■ **Keep things concrete.** Although third graders are perfectly capable of tackling rich and sometimes abstract content, they learn best when they're able to internalize this challenging learning through concrete means. For example, third graders are often asked to learn about different cultures and faraway places. Creating maps, drawing pictures, and designing posters about cultures they're studying from around the world can help students better take in information that is fairly abstract for them.

- **Keep things manageable.** Many third graders are very enthusiastic as they get excited about a project, and they can have great ideas about ways to make a project fun and rich. However, they often struggle with keeping projects bite-sized. Help third graders by breaking larger projects into small tasks and dividing up whole-class projects into smaller group ones.

- **Don't underestimate third graders.** Having just cautioned you about keeping things manageable, I also have to tell you that I've seen third graders write deep and moving poetry, put together and act out a complicated class play, and provide empathic and mature coaching to younger students. Be wary of the following mind-set: "My class can't even sit quietly through a math lesson. They could never handle a field trip (or cooking project, or small-group research projects, and so on)." Third graders will often rise to a challenge, and their ability to focus will increase as you support them in tackling a reasonable amount of more complicated and fun work.

Classroom Games

Whether it's a game planned as part of a lesson to directly teach, practice, or reinforce an academic concept, or a quick energizer added to help wake up a sleepy class, there's nothing like a good game. Playfulness and movement spark creativity, energy, and happiness. What follows are some considerations as you plan class games.

Make Time for Lively Learning

Going on a field trip, putting on a class musical, or even taking five minutes to play a game in the middle of the day. . . . With our packed school days, such things might seem like luxuries. When I find myself slipping into this mind-set, I remember a former colleague of mine. I would often pop my head in her doorway in the morning to ask a question: "Janie? Do you have a minute?" She would reply: "I don't have a minute, but for you, I will make a minute!"

This attitude is the key. Lively learning can't be optional or something we do when the other work is finished. Instead, we need to embed games and hands-on experiential learning throughout the day. These can replace some of the less-active learning activities that may already be in place.

For example, third graders often start memorizing math facts. We could have them sit still and practice timed math sheets. Or we could play some class games that involve skip counting and math facts. Students will likely be more engaged, have more positive energy, and be more successful if their math facts practice is lively and active.

Tailor the Game for the Moment

When the class has just finished a long period of quiet work (for example, a reading or writing workshop), a game that's fun and lively (and nonacademic) such as Simon Says might be just the thing to perk everyone up. As a transition from an active period to a quieter one, try a more relaxed game such as Twenty Questions or Hangman.

Keep It Quick

It can be tempting when playing games with students to let them go on a bit too long. Students are having fun and we're having fun. However, there can be too much of a good thing. A three-minute game might be enough to perk everyone up; a ten-minute game might result in students who become too silly to refocus.

Interactive Modeling

See Chapter 2, "Schedules and Routines," pages 34–37, for a full explanation of interactive modeling.

Teach Game-to-Work Transitions

Third graders are quite capable of making the transition from playing a silly game one minute to knuckling down for a quiet academic task the next, but they need to learn how.

Interactive modeling can be a great way to teach and practice the necessary skills. Have the class watch as you act out a silly game and then settle yourself back down. Be deliberate about showing how you do this (taking some deep breaths, closing your eyes for a few seconds, thinking about the next task, telling yourself that it's time to settle down, and so on). Have the class notice what you did and discuss various other strategies. Then give the class a challenge. Play a familiar game (for example, Simon Says) and see how quickly everyone can settle down at the end. If you bring out a stopwatch and time the transition, the transition itself can be a game!

Great Classroom Games to Try With Third Graders

■ **Pass the Pen.** Have the class stand in a circle with you. A volunteer steps into the middle of the circle. You name a category and begin passing a pen (or some other easy-to-handle object) around the circle. While the class races the pen around the circle, the student in the middle tries to name as many things as possible that fit in the category. The round ends when the pen gets back to the starting point. Try categories such as school staff members, favorite foods, and animals. More academic categories could be states, plants, outer space, fractions that are less than a half, or anything else from a current unit. Name a different category for each round to help students focus on fun rather than comparing how individuals did in relation to each other.

■ **No-Teeth Telephone.** Hand everyone in the class an index card with a word on it. (Pull vocabulary words out of the content you're teaching—science or social studies words, word wall words, math vocabulary, and so on) Begin with one student. This student says his or her "name" (the word on the card) twice and then calls someone else's "name" twice. For example, "Hexagon, hexagon, calling rhombus, rhombus." "Rhombus" then calls someone else: "Rhombus, rhombus, calling parallel lines, parallel lines." The game continues for as long as you'd like. The challenge of this game is that no one, whether speaking or not, is supposed to show their teeth. The game can be hysterically funny and also a great way to reinforce vocabulary words.

■ **Math Aerobics.** As students are practicing math problems, have them pick an exercise to do every time they finish a problem. One student might decide to do five jumping jacks every time she finishes a problem. Another student might do ten sit-ups. Yet another student might walk a lap around the classroom. You might be surprised at how well third graders can handle this kind of movement if it's set up carefully. Use interactive modeling to teach students exactly how to do these movements with self-control and without disturbing others who are still working.

74

Movement Isn't a Reward—It's a Basic Need

During my first year of teaching, I would occasionally try to coerce my class into working more by dangling the promise of extra recess in front of them. Eventually, I came to see that this was like tempting a marathon runner to go faster with a promise of a cup of water at the end of the race. Runners need to stay hydrated so they can run, just as learners need to stay active so they can focus and attend to tasks.

Learn More About Classroom Games at
www.responsiveclassroom.org

99 Activities and Greetings: Great for Morning Meetings . . . and other meetings, too! by Melissa Correa-Connolly (Northeast Foundation for Children, 2004).

Energizers! 88 Quick Movement Activities That Refresh and Refocus by Susan Lattanzi Roser (Northeast Foundation for Children, 2009).

Special Projects

One of my favorite things about third grade is that students are becoming much more independent in their reading and writing, and this enables them to engage in more complex and challenging projects. Independent research, creating a class movie, cooking a multicourse meal, and running a school store are just a few ideas for great third grade special projects. Here are some points to keep in mind when doing any kind of complex special project in third grade.

Gather Ideas From the Class

As you're diving into a new unit with third graders, it's great to have them brainstorm some fun ways to explore content and showcase their learning. But remember that although third graders can come up with incredible ideas when brainstorming as a class, these brainstorming sessions need to be managed well for them to be successful.

On the one hand, during brainstorming, you want to make sure students are feeling heard and their ideas are valued, so it's preferable to record their ideas on the brainstormed list "as is" whenever possible. On the other hand, sometimes ideas can start getting a bit off track, and this can snowball if not held in check by the teacher. We want to keep a brainstorming session focused and useful, but we need to avoid micromanaging and rephrasing too often, or students will feel manipulated.

Here are some tips to keep brainstorming sessions positive and productive:

- ■ **Give students a chance to prepare.** Students will be better able to participate in a brainstorming session if they have a chance to get ready. You might let them know in the morning that later in the day they'll be gathering ideas about possible field trips to learn about nature. Or you might begin the brainstorming session by having students partner chat about ideas.

■ **Set parameters.** When beginning a brainstorming list, make sure to set clear goals for the session. This will help students come up with ideas within the parameters that you expect. For example, instead of saying, "Let's brainstorm some fun favorite animals," which might be too open-ended, you could say, "Let's think of some possible class pets that can fit in a ten-gallon terrarium."

■ **Record ideas accurately.** When third graders give ideas in a brainstorming session, write their ideas word for word when you can. Sometimes it's necessary to paraphrase. When you do, make sure your rendition of their idea is correct. For example, a student might say, "I have an idea! Let's go to the science center down at the lake that has all of those tanks with lake animals in them!" You might ask, "Do you mean Echo Lake Science Center?" and then write "Visit Echo Lake Science Center" on the brainstorming chart.

■ **Redirect gently when necessary.** Although we want to encourage lots of different ideas, sometimes brainstorming sessions can become unhelpful if ideas get too grandiose, too specific, or unrealistic. For example, a student might say, "Florida is a short plane ride. Let's go to Busch Gardens to learn about animals!" You can tactfully redirect: "Busch Gardens is a great place to learn about animals. Right now, let's focus on places in our area."

■ **Let all voices be heard.** Let students know how you'll make sure they all have a chance to give an idea. You might say, "We're going to go around the circle and when it's your turn, you can share an idea. You may pass if you'd like." This can help third graders, who can be really concerned with fairness, focus more on their ideas and less on making sure they get a turn.

■ **Keep sessions short.** A few short brainstorming sessions are often more productive than one long one. Before you've exhausted all ideas, stop the session. "This is a great start to our list! I'm going to hang our chart on this wall so we can all keep thinking about these ideas. We'll put more ideas up when we come back in from lunch, so be ready to share!"

■ **Know when not to brainstorm.** You may already have a great idea for a fun project but worry that students won't be invested if they don't come up with the idea themselves. It might be tempting to have a brainstorming session where you try to lead them to the "right" option. This can be tricky, and students usually see right through what you're doing and feel manipulated. Instead, just tell them about your great idea. Chances are they'll be enthusiastic!

Try Partner Projects

Naturally gregarious, most third graders would work in large groups all the time if allowed to do so. But in my experience, partnerships are the most effective grouping choice for third graders when working on special projects. Two third graders working together can collaborate and cooperate effectively. Groups of three often mean that one student is left out or doesn't contribute enough to the group, and four or more students together often get overwhelmed by group management issues.

If you're going to allow larger cooperative groups, consider splitting children into partnerships within the groups or giving each student specific roles in the group. (Remember, each person's role needs to be modeled and practiced.)

Keep Work Bite-Sized

Third graders will tend to get really excited and then overzealous about their project work. Help them manage the process by breaking up big projects into smaller, bite-sized chunks. For example, let's say that two students are working on a research project on Japan as part of a larger class project on countries around the world. Creating a checklist of each phase of the process so they can keep track of incremental progress within the large project (see the sample on page 78) can help them stay focused without becoming overwhelmed.

Sample Project Checklist: Countries

Research Project Tasks	✔ When Complete
1. Choose country.	
Generate list of questions (at least 10).	
Collect first facts (at least 10).	
Meet with teacher.	
2. Collect next facts (at least 10).	
Meet with teacher.	
3. Ask new questions (at least 5).	
Collect last few facts.	
Organize facts using color coding.	
Meet with teacher.	
4. Generate list of project ideas.	
Describe project ideas (tell, write, or draw).	
Meet with teacher.	
5. Choose one project idea from list.	
Create project.	
Plan and practice presentation.	
Meet with teacher.	
6. Present project to the class.	
7. Fill out a self-evaluation.	

78

Learn More About Children's Research Projects at www.responsiveclassroom.org

The Research-Ready Classroom: Differentiating Instruction Across Content Areas by Mike Anderson and Andy Dousis (Heinemann, 2006).

Use Appropriate Assessments

Third graders can benefit from clear, concise, and concrete assessment tools that help them recognize things they've done well and help them set realistic goals for future work. The table on the opposite page shows the types of assignments to try and the types to avoid.

Assessing Third Graders

Suggested Assessments	Assessments to Avoid
■ **Checklists.** Students can simply check off project requirements as they complete them.	■ **Peer assessments.** Third graders shouldn't be placed in a situation where they have to assess one another. Let assessment remain the teacher's job.
■ **Rubrics.** Students can help create their own rubrics for what qualities or elements should be in their final projects.	■ **Letter grades.** Impersonal and often subjective, letter grades used in isolation give little information that students can use to improve their work.
■ **Self-assessments.** Teach students how to honestly appraise their own work (focusing on positives without ignoring challenges).	■ **One-word feedback.** Words such as "Great!" or "Sloppy" give children little to go on. Instead, offer specific assessments that reinforce the positives and offer suggestions for growth.
■ **Lists.** Bulleted lists of "things done well," coupled with one or two "suggestions for next time" can help encourage thoughtful reflection.	■ **√+, √, √−.** Like letter grades, check marks tend to be too general to offer valuable feedback.
■ **Narratives.** Writing a simple note or letter that highlights what a student did well and gives one or two ideas for improvement personalizes your feedback.	■ **Public assessments.** Students should not be assessed in front of others. Once they've done a presentation or shared their work, a private conference or paper-based assessment is more appropriate.

Give Choices

No matter what the content area, when students have choices about what or how they learn, they're more engaged and invested in their work. Some examples of choices:

■ **Collective class choices.** The class could discuss how they can best share their learning about plants with the rest of the school.

■ **Small-group choices.** Each group can decide which elements from the book they just read are most important to include in their skits.

■ **Individual choices.** Students could write a poem, newspaper article, or comic strip to show some of what they've learned in their study of Colonial America.

Field Trips

Field trips are an exciting event for any grade, and third graders are no exception. Often industrious and with increasing abilities to gather, organize, and process information, third graders are primed to take full advantage of the experiential learning opportunities that come with successful field trips.

Third graders are often eager and excited about going on field trips. Here are some tips to help keep them on track:

Set Up Groups Ahead of Time

No matter how compelling the content of the field trip, third graders will most likely be concerned initially about who is in their group. Spend time beforehand planning groups, or you'll be spending extra time during the field trip managing groups that are struggling.

Craft Groups With Friendships in Mind

You'll often find third graders gravitating toward their friends while on the trip, so unless you're okay with five small groups all morphing together into one big group, make sure that all students have at least one other good friend in whatever groups you create. They'll likely learn more if they're with friends, since if they're not, they're likely to spend a significant portion of their energy feeling upset—or trying to find and be with their friends!

Choose friendship groups wisely. If you know that three boys tend to giggle and get distracted when they're together, put each of them with other friends in separate groups. If a couple of students who are normally good friends are going through a rough time, keep them separate for the trip to help keep the peace. Consider keeping students who have not been getting along lately in different groups, especially if you're going to count on parent chaperones who may not know how to handle sticky situations.

Consider Same-Gender Groups

Field trips may not be the best time to make mixed-gender groups a priority. Because one of my goals when grouping children for field trips is to make sure they're comfortable enough in their groups to be able to learn effectively, I tend to create same-gender groups. If you do want to mix genders, I strongly recommend having small groups with at least two boys and two girls so that everyone has at least one same-gender buddy in the group.

Consider Creating Individual Jobs

When each student in a group has a particular task, each member can approach the field trip with industry and a sense of purpose. Here are some field trip jobs:

■ **Note Taker.** This person writes down important ideas for the group to remember.

■ **Question Asker.** This person can ask questions for the group.

■ **Folder Holder.** This person keeps track of the group's paperwork (schedule, notes, pamphlets, and so on).

■ **Picture Taker.** If the group has a digital camera, one person can hold the camera and take most of the pictures.

Of course, if one of your goals is to have everyone take notes, it wouldn't make sense to assign a note taker. And if everyone is going to want to do a certain job (for example, taking pictures), consider a way to rotate such jobs so that everyone gets a turn.

Structure Field Trips Appropriately

I've seen even the most patient and cooperative third graders fall apart on field trips that require too much sitting and listening and not enough doing. Many places that routinely host field trips for elementary school students don't adjust their programs according to the age they teach, so third graders may get the same program as sixth graders.

Talking ahead of time with the person hosting the field trip is often helpful. You might ask that students have opportunities to get up and move at least every ten minutes and have a chance to ask questions and handle materials as part of the presentation, instead of saving it all for the end. You might also suggest that partner chats be built into the sessions so that students will have a chance to talk with each other in ways that are appropriate and meaningful.

Plan Downtime

Third graders' tendency to tire quickly in normal settings can be more pronounced during field trips. Consider building in several rest breaks throughout the day. You may even need to require students to sit down for a few minutes so they can maintain their stamina later on. Bringing along a

Think About Food and Bathroom Needs

Food and bathroom "emergencies" can sneak up on students during a field trip. Third graders are often so engaged in what they're doing that they don't feel these needs building, so consider the following ideas.

■ **Food breaks.** Schedule a couple of short snack breaks throughout the trip to keep students awake and lively.

■ **Drinks.** Third graders will often exert immense amounts of energy if they walk or run around a lot. They dehydrate quickly on a hot day, so make sure there's water handy.

■ **Bathroom breaks.** Make sure you know where the bathrooms are located wherever you're going. Plan on bringing the whole class to bathrooms before getting on the bus, when you arrive at the site, during or after lunch, and before you get on the bus to return to school. (Also make sure chaperones know what to do if a student throws up or has a bathroom emergency.)

fun read-aloud can be a great way to give students a few minutes to rest and recover in the middle of a busy day away from school. It can also lend some semblance of normalcy when everything else during the day is so different.

Discuss Field Trip Goals

Students need a chance to use the information and learning they acquire on the trip in a productive way. Perhaps you'll create a bulletin board as a class, highlighting work done and pictures taken. You might form teams of students who will prepare short presentations to share their learning with other classes. Or perhaps the learning students bring back is part of a larger project (class play, class research project, and so on) within a science or social studies unit. Whatever the case, make sure students know the goals of the trip before they go—they'll focus more on the learning of the trip if they do.

Give Structured Learning Tasks

Field trips with third graders run more smoothly and are more purposeful if we give them fun learning tasks to accomplish while they're on their trip. This means giving simple and meaningful work for students to do that won't feel burdensome or like busy-work. You might also present a few tasks to students and let them choose the one(s) they most want to do. When you return from the trip, these work samples can be proudly displayed on a class bulletin board.

Ideas for Learning Tasks for Field Trips

- Make a list of interesting information you learn on our trip.

- Draw a few sketches to share some of what you learn.

- Create a list of questions that you thought about on our trip.

- Here's a checklist of things you may see. Check them off as you find them. Be ready to tell about your favorite!

Consider giving students simple recording sheets for each of these ideas.

Anticipate Behavior Changes

When students go on a field trip, their behaviors may change for many reasons: the change in routines, different energy levels of other students, teacher anxiety, having parent chaperones, and so on. As much as possible, be proactive with the class about how to behave appropriately on a trip:

assign seats on the bus, put the most challenging students in your own group, and make sure everyone's getting enough food and water and bathroom and rest breaks.

Still, you should anticipate that some students may have a challenging time with behavior. So make sure to have a backup plan in case things go awry. Be ready to pull students out of their group if their behaviors are getting in the way of others' learning. Know who might be able to sit with a student who needs a quiet break from the group. Be ready to head off small behavior challenges (silly giggling at an inappropriate time, kicking up dust while walking on a trail, or asking intentionally off-track questions of a speaker) before they mushroom into much bigger problems that require more serious interventions.

Bring Each Field Trip to a Thoughtful Close

My first couple of years of teaching, once a field trip was over, I'd be thrilled if I actually came home with the right number of students and no one threw up. We'd get off the bus, head back to the room, and that was the end of it. But I quickly learned that if field trips are to be not only fun excursions but actual learning tasks, we need to thoughtfully conclude each field trip.

First of all, we need to make sure students know what to do as soon as they're off the bus. Make sure they know where to go, where to put their things, and how to walk quietly in the hallways. If left unguided, students may run (loudly) through the hallways, toss their backpacks on the floor, and start play-wrestling around the room.

Second, you'll want to remind students about the projects they'll be working on based on the trip. Right after they return is a great time for silently writing down ideas individually, since everything will still be fresh in their minds.

Closing Thoughts

Class field trips, classroom games, and special projects are all vitally important learning tasks for third graders. All give students a chance to be fully and deeply engaged in meaningful and enjoyable work. At any given time of the year, exciting and fun learning projects like these should be going on.

At the same time, we have to be careful not to overload ourselves and students with too much of a good thing. We should balance intense projects with more routine work. If we're doing a big cooking project as part of a social studies unit, we might rely on the math book to get us through math lessons for a couple of weeks. If we're prepping for standardized testing and don't have time or space in the room for a big project, a series of fun games each day to reinforce content and keep people moving might be enough.

When we take care not to overwhelm ourselves and students with too many big projects at once, the ones we do take on will likely be more successful and leave us with the positive energy we'll need for the next activity.

CHAPTER 5

Communicating With Parents

This year, as our son, Ethan, entered third grade, Heather and I were a bit nervous. Third grade was feeling like a "big kid" age in our house, and we had lots of questions about what Ethan's third grade experience would be like. Fortunately, his teacher is a fantastic communicator. She contacted all parents and students over the summer to give some basic information about the upcoming year. She held an informal and very friendly open house night a couple of days before school started so our whole family could go in with Ethan, meet her, and check out his classroom. As the year has moved along, his teacher continues to keep us updated with frequent and easy-to-understand information about upcoming events (such as field trips and standardized testing) and daily classroom life. Heather and I really appreciate knowing what's going on in Ethan's classroom. We now feel much more relaxed about having a third grader!

Effective communication with families is important at any grade, and third grade is no exception. It can be a big transition year for children. Students start reading more independently, they're able to read and write longer stories and texts, science and social studies begin to play a more prominent role in the school day, and bigger projects start to take shape. All of these changes can be exciting and amazing for parents to watch, but parents often have lots of questions as well. "How's Gina doing in writing this

About the Term "Parent"

Students come from a variety of homes with a variety of family structures. Many children are being raised by grandparents, siblings, aunts and uncles, and foster families. All of these people are to be honored for devoting their time, attention, and love to raising children. Coming up with one word that encompasses all these caregivers is challenging. For simplicity's sake, this book uses the word "parent" to refer to anyone who is the child's primary caregiver.

year? I see that she's spelling lots of words wrong." "How much time should Mikel be spending on homework? He seems to rush through it in a couple of minutes. Is he doing okay?" "I want to come in and help out in the class like I did in second grade. Can I still do that?"

When we forge effective lines of communication with parents, we're able to share information about what and how students are doing in school and learn important information about how things are going outside of school. As a result, we can better meet each student's needs.

Strategies for Good Communication

Share Positive News About Each Child

Starting at the beginning of the year and continuing regularly throughout the year, send messages to parents about strengths you observe in their child. It's important for families to hear from you when their child is doing fine, not just when he or she needs to get back on track. When parents hear positive information about their child and know that you're seeing things that are going well, they're more likely to communicate with you when they have a question and more likely to be approachable if you need to broach a difficult topic.

Learn More About Working with Families of Different Cultures at www.responsiveclassroom.org

Parents & Teachers Working Together by Carol Davis and Alice Yang (Northeast Foundation for Children, 2005).

- **Welcome letter.** Introduce yourself to families and let them know a bit about the upcoming year. Be careful not to overwhelm parents with too much information in this first communication. The best tone to take is a light and purposeful one that lets parents feel comfortable about getting in touch with you. Make sure to include contact information so they know how to reach you. (See the sample letter on the opposite page.)

- **Informal classroom visits before school starts.** If you can, give parents and students a time to come in and check out the room and meet you informally. It might be a day when you're planning on working in the room anyway, or it might be a two-hour block some evening before the year begins. During family visits, consider a quick activity for people to do (a simple scavenger hunt for the student's desk or cubby, for the caterpillars on a shelf, and so forth) in case many families visit at once and some

CONTINUED ON PAGE 90

Sample Letter to Parents

Dear Parents and Caregivers,

Welcome to third grade! I am really looking forward to our upcoming year together. Third grade is an exciting year for students and parents, and I'd like to give you a little information about the beginning of the year.

First, let me introduce myself briefly. I've been teaching for fifteen years in third, fourth, and fifth grades. I've been here at our school since 1999. When I'm not in school, I love to spend time with my wife, Heather, and our two children, Ethan and Carly.

This year our class will be exploring a lot of exciting topics. In science, we'll learn about plants and ecology, the solar system, weather, and geology. In social studies, we'll learn about cultures from around the world, geography, and government. In math, we're going to dive into multiplication, geometry, fractions, and many other exciting topics. In literacy, we'll be having reading workshop and writing workshop. I've planned some fun units in personal experience narratives, reading and writing short nonfiction texts, and fiction. You'll be amazed at how much reading and writing your student will do this year!

As the year begins, we'll also spend some time learning classroom routines and getting to know each other. As we explore new learning topics and review some content from second grade, we'll also work at becoming a strong community together. When students feel safe and comfortable in their classrooms, they're better able to take on academic challenges.

In a few weeks, we'll have our annual Back to School Night. Here's something you can start thinking about for that evening: What are your hopes for your third grader this year in school? What kinds of academic and social goals do you have for your child? I look forward to hearing your thoughts.

Please contact me if you have any questions. You can email me at mr_anderson@school.org or call me at home anytime before 8:00 PM (XXX-XXX-XXXX). I'm looking forward to meeting you and to a great year!

need to wait to chat with you. Or invite students to pick out a book to read on the first day of school. Knowing at least one thing they'll be doing can be comforting for many children.

■ **Phone calls and email.** During the first week or two of school, contact each parent to share something positive about their child. "Hi! This is Mr. Anderson. I just wanted to let you know that Cam has had a great start to the year. He's been reading some *Magic Tree House* books during reading time, and he's really enjoying the insect collections we've been doing in science."

Emailing Parents

In general, serious or confidential matters are best discussed in person, by phone, or in a paper-and-envelope letter. But email can be great for quick notes about day-to-day classroom life. A few things to consider:

■ **Know if parents can—and want to—use email.** At the fall open house, invite parents to sign up to receive email from you if they'd like. Tell them you'll also be communicating in other ways. Judge by the number of sign-ups whether to use email regularly.

■ **Keep the volume of messages manageable by communicating in other ways.** Most parents rely less on email once they know you'll be sharing news in various ways.

■ **Follow the guidelines.** Check whether your school, district, or parent organization has guidelines for emailing families.

90

■ **Formal open house.** Most schools host some sort of formal Back to School Night during the first few weeks of school. These are great chances to help parents learn about the upcoming school year and to answer some common third grade questions ("How much homework will there be?" "What is your spelling program like?"). Keep the tone professional and easygoing. If you have a lot of information to give parents, consider sharing some highlights out loud and providing written information with more details. If this is the first time some parents have been in the classroom, build in some time for them to explore. Make sure they can see some of their child's work and where their child sits. Parents like to have a picture of what their child's day is like!

■ **Website.** If your school has a website with a page for each teacher, you might post a general introduction to the year when school starts and then update the page with new information about classroom events and work throughout the year. Make sure to send everyone an email or note with a link to the site when you make a major change or addition. (Find out your school's or district's guidelines for class websites.)

Listen

Parents are experts on their own children and have a lot of valuable insights to offer that will help you better teach their child. When we communicate with parents, we need to make sure we spend time listening. Parents can help us understand how to help their children in school by offering important information about how things are going outside of school. Make sure to build time into conversations to ask parents what ideas and questions they have.

Empathize

When students are struggling with schoolwork or friendship issues at school, parents can be understandably upset. A very wise teacher once helped me understand that often, although parents express their concerns using angry tones of voice and facial expressions, their anger is rooted in fear. They're afraid for their child. We'll react with greater empathy if we keep that in mind, and we'll tend to be less defensive and better able to focus on possible solutions.

Do Parents Have Literacy or Language Issues?

Be on the lookout for indications that students' parents have difficulty reading. If they do, be careful about relying on written information too often. Look for other ways to communicate, such as phone calls or recorded messages that parents can call in to receive.

For example, a parent might confront you in a loud and accusatory tone at an open house night, "Why hasn't there been any spelling homework yet? It's already the third week of school! Don't you care about spelling?" Instead of reacting with anger or frustration, you might reply, "It sounds like spelling is a really important topic that we should talk about. I'm eager to share with you how we'll be working on spelling this year in third grade."

Communicate Regularly and Consistently

My first couple of years teaching, I didn't update parents nearly often enough about what we were doing in school. I tended to count on students to tell their parents what was happening. We were doing such cool stuff, after all, that I assumed children were running off the school bus shouting to their parent, "Guess what we did in science today?"

It's still my hope that children are so excited about what's going on in class that they'll rush off the bus eager to share, and this does, in fact, sometimes happen. However, by the time the bus rolls to a stop, the children may have already had at least twenty-five interactions and events that have taken precedence over the cool experiment they conducted that afternoon in science. So primarily counting on students to communicate with parents about daily school events was a bit naïve on my part. If you want parents to have a good idea of what's going on at school, it's best to send home frequent communications yourself. Here are some tips:

■ **Be brief.** Parents generally prefer frequent short updates. Most adults are tired at the end of a long day, so a double-sided, single-spaced letter is likely to be put aside.

■ **Be consistent.** If you're going to send home weekly updates, do it on the same day each week so parents know to expect it. Consider using the same method almost all of the time (for example, emails and newsletters) so parents don't have to keep track of too many kinds of communication.

■ **Be positive and upbeat.** Even when communicating about a class challenge, keep your tone positive. For example, if the class isn't great at bringing back permission slips or homework papers, you might say, "One challenge we're tackling as a class right now is remembering to bring things back to school. We've started collecting some ideas and are having a class meeting on Friday to pick one idea to try. It's tough for us right now, but we'll get better!"

Share Information About Child Development

The more we can help parents understand child development, the better. Parents will know that we're mindful of developmental issues as we decide how best to support their student's learning. They'll also better understand their growing and changing child.

Here are some ideas to communicate to parents:

■ **Rates of growth differ among children.** Human growth and development is complex, and no two children reach a particular milestone at the same time. For example, although third grade is often a time when children begin to read with great fluency, some children may have hit that milestone much earlier, while others may still be progressing in that area.

■ **Physical, cognitive, and social growth rates may differ.** Though a child might be tall for her age, she may appear "young" socially. A child who is struggling with simple subtraction may be able to work cooperatively with a variety of different personality types and help solve disputes in ways that seem quite advanced.

■ **Children will change as the year progresses.** A student who begins the year outgoing and eager to try anything (a common third grade characteristic) may end it showing more caution and sensitivity (more common fourth grade traits).

Child Development Resources for Parents at www.responsiveclassroom.org

Yardsticks: Children in the Classroom Ages 4–14 by Chip Wood (Northeast Foundation for Children, 2007), or the child development pamphlets based on this book.

Another Resource:

How To Talk So Kids Will Listen and Listen So Kids Will Talk by Adele Faber and Elaine Mazlish (Harper, 1999).

■ **Growth often happens in fits and starts.** Many parents recognize that children's physical growth happens through growth spurts followed by lulls. Cognitive, language, and social aspects of development often happen this way, too. Reading development is a great example. Students often make great gains in a short amount of time and then seem to need some time to practice and consolidate their new skills before making another dramatic leap.

■ **Third graders tend to be enthusiastic but may lack focus.** Parents may be confused when they see their child get really excited about the idea of taking piano lessons one week and then drop the idea the next. Or they might see their child start building an elaborate city out of cereal and shoe boxes on a Saturday morning and then find the materials abandoned as the child runs off to another adventure. This is pretty common among third graders. Parents can help their child put sustained effort into projects they choose to do at home by participating with them (helping them write the script for the play they want to perform for their grandparents, for example) or guiding them in choosing one after-school activity and sticking to it.

■ **Third grade is a year of immense growth.** Sometimes parents hear about all the learning activities that will go on in third grade and worry that their child may not be ready. Assure parents that you'll keep learning projects reasonable and that they'll be amazed by what their child will be able to do by the spring!

93

Let Parents Know How They Can Help

If you want parents to volunteer for field trips, lend a hand with special projects, or help out with math games, let them know this at the beginning of the year. Another way that parents can help their child is by making sure their child is eating healthy foods and getting enough sleep. Because third graders are starting to look and act more like "big kids," parents may forget how young they still are and how much sleep they need. Remind parents that getting enough sleep and eating healthy foods are incredibly important for children who need to be able to work and play hard all day at school.

Ask Parents If They'd Like to Share a Skill or Interest

Many teachers send a survey to parents early in the year asking if they have a special interest or talent they'd like to share with the class. Storytelling, woodworking, quilting—parents can offer a wide variety of exciting experiences for the class, beyond what you can provide by yourself. Inviting this sort of participation not only honors parents, but also enriches the curriculum.

Special Concerns of Third Grade Parents

Three main questions seem to come up again and again among third grade parents. Knowing that these are likely to be issues will help you craft thoughtful responses.

Writing

"Her writing is messy." "There are too many spelling mistakes." "He always forgets capital letters." "Her stories don't make sense!" These all might be concerns you hear from parents of third graders. Although elements such as voice, story development, and creativity are important in writing, parents understandably want their child to do well in spelling, handwriting, capitalization, paragraphing, and other basic details as well. They may also notice that their child seems much better with reading than with writing, and that might seem troubling. You can help allay parents' worries by explaining the following:

■ **It's okay for children to be stronger readers than writers in third grade.** Remind parents about how children acquire language. Children can understand most of what they hear before they can verbalize it. Likewise, in third grade a similar gap may exist between reading and writing development. A child may be able to read surprisingly challenging chapter books, but his writing may still be catching up.

■ **Many third graders start to write more.** Many children, regardless of the quality of their writing, are suddenly writing much more in third grade. In second grade, they might have written a few sentences at a time, but in third grade, they start measuring the length of their stories in pages. Third graders also tend to write quickly, rushing to get all of their ideas down before they forget them.

■ **Mistakes are part of the writing process.** As they write longer pieces, play with new vocabularies, and develop the increased fine motor control that allows them to write more quickly, students will naturally make more mistakes. Asking third graders to write neatly and pay careful attention to spelling as they create first drafts can inhibit their writing. Messiness and spelling errors are part of the writing process. Reassure parents that writing errors will be addressed later (for example, when the focus is on editing and revising).

> **Is There Something to Parents' Worries?**
>
> At the same time that you're reassuring parents about their child's friendships or moods, observe the child (during recess, if necessary) to make sure there isn't a serious problem. If you see any worrisome signs, talk to your school or district guidance counselor, psychologist, or social worker for advice on next steps.

Progress

Social studies tests, science projects, graded report cards, multiplication facts, and writing in paragraphs are just a few examples of things third graders may be encountering that parents didn't see in second grade. All of a sudden, school can look much more serious to parents. At the same time, parents may be getting standardized test results and report cards that appear to give inconsistent information. Their child may be saying he or she is really good in math but bringing home math tests that seem to show otherwise. School personnel may be using jargon that parents don't fully understand, such as DRAs, QRIs, and IEPs.

"So, how is my child *doing*?" the confused parent may ask. We need to be ready to help parents get a clear picture.

■ **Explain conflicting data.** "I know your child didn't appear to do well on the math portion of the standardized test. Let me show you how he's doing in our math curriculum. Here's his last math test; it shows that he really understands these three skills in measurement. This last skill that he was struggling with was hard for the whole class, but the children are supposed to be at only a 'beginning' level of understanding in third grade. We don't expect mastery of this skill until fourth grade."

■ **Be clear, honest, and positive with parents.** "Ava is exactly where a third grader should be with reading right now. It's really common for third graders to read fluently but still struggle with comprehension. Reading for meaning is the next big skill we're going to work on together." Or, "William is struggling with math right now. At this point in the year, third graders are expected to add two-digit numbers. He and I are spending some extra time together on that concept."

Homework

Homework can be a difficult balancing act for parents, students, and teachers alike. How much does homework add to a child's learning? Does homework really teach what it's meant to teach? What should a parent's role be when a student is struggling with homework? Regardless of teachers' individual beliefs about homework, we all work in schools and districts that have policies regarding this aspect of school. The following tips can help make homework run more smoothly for third graders and their families.

■ **Keep homework bite-sized.** A little bit of homework each night that students can do independently is best. Keeping assignments short and manageable will help students feel successful with homework and keep stress low. Avoid large homework packets or long-term projects. These will often overwhelm third graders, who usually aren't ready to independently handle complicated time management tasks.

■ **Assign purposeful and interesting work.** "Collect a list of right angles you find around your home. We'll create a bulletin board showing what everyone found." "Make a list of at least five of your favorite TV shows and movies. We'll use this list in our writing workshop tomorrow." "Choose two multiplication facts you need to practice. Here are three different ways to practice them. Choose one way and practice for five minutes. Be ready to share how it went." These are just a few ideas about how to make homework feel less like busy work and more like meaningful and fun preparation for the next day's learning.

Homework Help at www.responsiveclassroom.org

"Homework Blues?" *Responsive Classroom News-letter*, Fall 2003.

"Homework! Strategies to overcome the struggles and help all students." *Responsive Classroom News-letter*, Fall 2000.

"Is Homework Working?" *Responsive Classroom Newsletter*, January 2006.

Another Resource:

Rethinking Homework: Best Practices that Support Diverse Needs by Cathy Vatterott (ASCD, 2009).

■ **Give clear written directions.** When assigning homework, make sure to pass out clear written directions. Avoid having third graders copy down assignments. This extra task can be quite challenging for many third graders, making it harder for them to be successful with homework.

■ **Teach and practice homework skills.** Consider using the first few weeks of the school year to teach students how to do homework. Talk about good times of day to do homework. Practice writing names and dates in the appropriate place on papers. Model and practice how to put homework away in a backpack and how to pass it in the next day. Practice how to read directions effectively. You can even have students do "homework" at school for the first few weeks until they gain confidence.

■ **Communicate with parents about their role in homework.** How can parents best support their child when it comes to homework? Help their child pick a good time and place? Check the homework before it goes into the backpack? Let their child be completely responsible for her or his own work? However you think parents can best help, make sure to communicate this message to them clearly and often. Also, let parents know how you'll be assessing homework and what your goals are for homework throughout the year. The more clearly parents understand how homework

works, the better they can appropriately support their children.

■ **Keep homework in perspective.** For some students, completing homework assignments at home can be challenging. Some students may be going back and forth from one parent or caregiver to another throughout the week and may frequently lose track of the contents of their backpacks as a result. Other children, even as young as third grade, may have to help take care of younger siblings, or they may not have a good place or time to get homework done. Be careful not to let homework take too large a role in how students view their own success. Children shouldn't feel like failures in school if they struggle with homework.

Hosting Productive Parent-Teacher Conferences

Parent-teacher conferences are amazing opportunities to have meaningful communication with families about their children. Parents know so much about their children that can help us better understand how to teach them effectively, and parents are often eager for news about how the school year is going. These conferences can be stressful for both teachers and parents, however. Especially for parents who didn't have great school experiences themselves, or for parents of children with social or academic challenges, coming in to meet with their child's teacher can be uncomfortable. Here are some suggestions for how to keep these conversations positive and productive:

Offer Conversation Starters

Having a few questions for parents can help ease you into a productive conversation: "What are your child's favorite things to do at school?" "What does she like to do outside of school?" "What are some things he's enjoying about school so far this year?" "What are some of your hopes and goals for this coming school year for your child?" If it seems appropriate, you can send these questions home before the conference so that parents have time to think about how they might answer them.

Invite Parents to Share Their Thoughts

Avoid talking at parents. Let them voice their ideas and opinions and give them a chance to ask questions. Parents often have valuable insights and thoughts about their children, and we need to make sure to hear them. "Tell me what you think" or "I'm curious as to what you've noticed" are simple ways to help parents share their thoughts during a conference.

Highlight the Positives First

All children have strengths and positive attributes, and any conference will be more productive and positive when we start by noting these attributes. If a child is facing challenges, you might be tempted to launch right into talking about those challenges, but doing so can set a negative tone for the conference and push parents into a defensive mode. Consider the following positive example: "Sasha's writing has such amazing voice and strength. The ideas that she comes up with in her stories are often unique and quite advanced for third grade. Our next challenge is to help her finish a piece. Her stories seem to start out strongly, and then she often drops them to start something else. It's important for Sasha to bring a writing piece to completion, so that's our next goal for her in writing."

Tackle Only One or Two Issues

Some students may have many challenges, but we have to be careful not to overwhelm parents with too many concerns at once. Remember, you have all year to work with students and their families, so don't feel that you have to work on everything right away. Instead, begin simply by highlighting only one or two issues and suggesting ways that families can help out. For example, a student might be struggling with several academic issues, including remembering subtraction facts. During the parent–teacher conference, after highlighting some positives, you might share a fun math game that the family can play together to reinforce subtraction facts.

Let Parents Know If You Need Time to Think

Every now and then, parents will raise an issue or ask a question that you need time to think about. If so, try simply letting the parent know that instead of giving a hasty response. "That's an interesting observation. I'd like to take some time to observe David in the classroom for a few days. Let me call you on Friday and I'll share what I notice." Let the parents know when you'll get back in touch with them, and then make sure to follow through.

Be Flexible

Sometimes your carefully crafted plans for a conference will need to be ditched. I'll never forget when a parent sat down for a meeting and burst into tears. "My wife of eighteen years just left me, and I'm lost without her!" he cried. A bit stunned, I sat and listened while handing him tissues and letting him know that I would do my best to help his son through this difficult family time. If you're thrown a curveball like this, be empathic and understanding while also trying to get the conference refocused on the child. Sometimes that may be impossible, so in a worst-case scenario just remember that you can always have another conference at another time.

Involving Parents in Events and Activities

Having parents join your classroom for everyday activities and special events can be a wonderful way to strengthen home–school connections for students. It can also be a way for the class to take on more involved activities that you might not be able to manage on your own. Remember the following ideas for helping parents have successful visits in the classroom.

Set Expectations for Parents

Just like students, parents need to know the classroom rules. Otherwise, they'll sometimes break the rules without meaning to. For example, they might talk with each other during a lesson. This can be confusing for students. To help parents follow rules, consider sending the rules to them before they come in to volunteer. You might also have copies posted or ready to hand out as parents arrive. (See page 102 for a sample.)

Maintain Consistent Discipline

Children often act differently when their parents are around. Whether parents are volunteering in the classroom or taking part in a school event with their child outside of school hours, make sure to hold students to the same classroom rules as always. The chart on the next page shows some behaviors you might see and some ways you could respond.

When Children Misbehave During Family Visits

Situation	What You Might Say or Do
Chris is a naturally bubbly and energetic third grader, but when his mom comes in to help with a cooking project, his behavior becomes exaggerated. He uses a loud voice and tells silly jokes that distract his group.	"Chris, your group is having a hard time following directions right now. Come sit with me for a few minutes until you're calm. Then you can rejoin your group."
Ben has worked hard at becoming more independent in third grade, but when his father comes in to help with bookmaking, he regresses. Ben wants his dad to tie his shoes, sharpen his pencil, and get him a tissue.	"Ben, you know how to do those things on your own. You take care of your jobs so your dad can take care of the bookmaking."
Lauren is often quick with an insult or a shove on the playground, but she's working hard to use kind, friendly behavior. When her aunt comes in to share recess games with the class, Lauren's behavior gets more aggressive.	"Lauren, come take a break with me." Once she's cooled off a bit, continue in a calm voice. "I know it can be hard when different adults are running games at recess. You can either play safely or watch. Which would you rather do?"

Keep Groups Small

Whether you're organizing children for a project in the classroom or for a field trip, create groups that family volunteers can handle. Most parents don't have the skills needed to manage discipline problems, so keep groups to four students or fewer and assign students who struggle with self-control to your own group.

Give Parents Nonteaching Roles

In my first year of teaching, I decided to have parents help out with writing conferences during writing workshop. Even though I had given parents pointers ahead of time on how to conduct these conferences, I heard parents focusing on misspelled words ("Just sound it out!") and saw them writing all over student drafts. I soon realized that I couldn't expect nonteachers to pick up the skill of effective conferencing so quickly. Better to give parents important but nonteaching jobs such as using a hot glue gun, binding poetry anthologies, or helping cut out pieces for an art project.

Involve All Parents

Some parents have a hard time coming in to school. Past negative experiences with school, inflexible work schedules, cultural or language barriers, and young children at home who require constant care are just some possible reasons. Some parents might just feel that they don't have anything to offer. But all students benefit from family involvement in school, so it's up

---

Sample Guidelines for Parent Volunteers

Thanks for volunteering in our classroom! Here are some guidelines and information to help you out:

Class Routines

- **Hand signal/chime.** When I raise my hand or ring the chime, that's our class signal to stop working and look at me. Adults can help by doing the same.

- **Bathroom sign-out.** Students may sign out to use the bathroom on their own. They can help explain our process if you have questions.

Volunteer Guidelines

- **Adult voice.** Adult voices can sometimes carry farther than we think. When working with a student (or a small group), make sure to use a quiet voice so others can stay focused on their work.

- **Discipline.** If a student is refusing to do work or being at all disruptive, let me know and I will handle the situation.

- **Privacy.** As a volunteer in our classroom, you may see a student struggling. Please respect the privacy of all students by not discussing student-related issues outside of our classroom.

- **Anything else.** If you have any questions at all, please let me know.

to us to encourage all families to participate in some way. Here are some ideas for how we can do that:

- **Have families share their culture with the class.** One year for our holiday celebration, our class hosted a solstice luncheon in our room. Families brought in a favorite food that represented their family or their culture. This event brought into the classroom many parents who hadn't yet visited.

- **Host events in the evening.** This way, parents who can't join the class during the school day might be able to participate.

- **Send out a special call for help.** For example, if a field trip is coming up, send a special note to families asking for participation. "Dear Parents, We have a field trip to the aquarium coming up, and we need chaperones. If you haven't joined our class for activities yet—or even if you have!—this would be a great opportunity to spend some time with us."

- **Keep costs low.** If parents have to pay money to participate in an event, find a way to keep the costs low so that families strapped for cash don't feel left out. Make sure most opportunities for family involvement don't require any money at all.

- **Let parents know when siblings can attend.** Especially for families with very young children, it's always nice to know when they can bring along little ones.

Closing Thoughts

Third graders, like students in any grade, benefit when their teachers and families work together. Like other elementary students, third graders usually also love having their families involved in school. When we take the time to build effective parent–teacher relationships, everyone wins. Proactive and thoughtful communication helps ensure a successful year for us, for parents, and most importantly, for our students.

Favorite Books, Board Games, and Websites

for Third Graders

If you're new to third grade, chances are that building a classroom library and a collection of grade-appropriate games and websites is on your to-do list. My goal in this appendix is to give you a starting point—options to consider in different categories. These lists are not meant to be definitive. And please note that many items on the lists represent some of my own personal favorites, which may or may not suit your tastes and needs. But I hope you'll find a few ideas and resources here that will help you get started!

105

Read-Aloud Books

Because of Winn-Dixie
by Kate DiCamillo

The BFG by Roald Dahl

The Birchbark House by Louise Erdrich

The Enormous Egg by Oliver Butterworth

Frindle by Andrew Clements

How to Eat Fried Worms
by Thomas Rockwell

How Many Seeds in a Pumpkin?
by Margaret McNamara,
illustrated by G. Brian Karas

The Hundred Penny Box
by Sharon Bell Mathis

In Our Mothers' House by Patricia Polacco

Jin Woo by Eve Bunting,
illustrated by Chris K. Soentpiet

The Lorax by Dr. Seuss

Marco's Monster by Meredith Sue Willis

Ramona Quimby, Age 8 by Beverly Cleary

Snapshots from the Wedding by Gary Soto,
illustrated by Stephanie Garcia

The Tale of Despereaux
by Kate DiCamillo

The Trumpet of the Swan by E. B. White

Virgie Goes to School with Us Boys
by Elizabeth Fitzgerald Howard,
illustrated by E. B. Lewis

Classroom Library Books

All of the read-alouds listed previously are also great for the classroom library. In addition, consider some of these titles:

Series Fiction

Books written in a series are a must-have for third grade classroom libraries. As third graders work at building fluency, series books keep many things, such as characters, themes, and story lines, predictable while helping readers feel competent, energized, and excited about reading.

The Adventures of the Bailey School Kids by Marcia Thornton and Debbie Dadey

The American Girls Collection by multiple authors

The A to Z Mysteries by Ron Roy

Cam Jansen by David A. Adler

Dunc and Amos by Gary Paulsen

Geronimo Stilton by Geronimo Stilton (a mouse!)

Horrible Harry by Suzy Kline

Judy Moody by Megan McDonald

The Littles by John Peterson

The Magic School Bus (chapter books and picture books) by multiple authors and illustrators

Magic Tree House by Mary Pope Osborne

The Secrets of Droon by Tony Abbott

The Time Warp Trio by Jon Scieszka

Fiction Authors

Another great way to help third graders find books they'll love is by having collections of books by particular authors. Many third graders get hooked on favorite authors the same way they get hooked on favorite series. These authors have written many books that are great for third grade classroom libraries.

Joseph Bruchac

Beverly Cleary

Andrew Clements

Matt Christopher

Roald Dahl

Demi

Virginia Hamilton

Pat Mora

Gary Paulsen

Dav Pilkey

Faith Ringgold

Poetry

all the small poems and fourteen more
by Valerie Worth

Joyful Noise: Poems for Two Voices
by Paul Fleischman

A Light in the Attic by Shel Silverstein

My Dog May Be a Genius
by Jack Prelutsky

Ordinary Things by Ralph Fletcher

Stone Soup magazine

Where the Sidewalk Ends
by Shel Silverstein

Informational Texts and Nonfiction

Childhood of Famous Americans series
from Aladdin Paperbacks

Eye Wonder Books from
DK Publishing

Eyewitness Books from DK Publishing

Highlights magazine

Nature's Wild series from Advance
Publishers

Ranger Rick magazine

Adding to Your Class or School Library

To find additional books and authors, talk with other teachers, librarians, parents—and the children themselves. These websites are also a great resource for expanding any library:

New York Public Library:
Best Books for Children
KIDS.NYPL.ORG/READING/RECOMMENDED.CFM

Association for Library Service to Children (ALSC):
Caldecott Medal Books
WWW.ALA.ORG/ALA/MGRPS/DIVS/ALSC/AWARDSGRANTS/BOOKMEDIA/
CALDECOTTMEDAL/CALDECOTTMEDAL.CFM

National Council for the Social Studies (NCSS):
Notable Tradebooks for Young People
WWW.SOCIALSTUDIES.ORG/RESOURCES/NOTABLE

Board and Card Games

Checkers	Parcheesi
Connect 4 (Hasbro)	Rummikub (Pressman)
Dominoes	Slamwich (Gamewright)
Mancala	Spill and Spell (Endless Games)
Othello	UNO (Mattel)
Pay Day (Winning Moves Games)	Yahtzee (Hasbro)

Websites

Exploring Nature Educational Resource ■ WWW.EXPLORINGNATURE.ORG
Provides reference sources on science topics and includes worksheets, flashcards, and other materials.

Funbrain ■ WWW.FUNBRAIN.COM Offers a variety of interactive games across subject areas.

National Geographic Kids ■ WWW.KIDS.NATIONALGEOGRAPHIC.COM
Includes a variety of interactive games about science and math.

Math Is Fun! ■ WWW.MATHISFUN.COM Provides information about math and interactive math games.

netTrekker ■ WWW.NETTREKKER.COM Search engine for science and social studies research. Requires a subscription.

VocabularySpellingCity ■ WWW.SPELLINGCITY.COM Creates games, worksheets, and quizzes based upon the spelling list a child enters.

Time for Kids ■ WWW.TIMEFORKIDS.COM Kid-friendly news and learning games.

ACKNOWLEDGMENTS

Can anyone out there really write a book all on their own? If there are such people, I'm certainly not one of them! A lot of people contributed to this book, both directly and indirectly, and I'd like to thank as many of them as I can.

My career as an elementary school teacher has been filled with many wonderful colleagues and administrators who have helped shape my beliefs about teaching elementary school and my teaching practices. I'd like to thank the many friends and colleagues at both Flanders Elementary School and Dondero Elementary School who have helped and inspired me over the years. You have helped me learn and understand the powers of observing children and being self-reflective about my teaching.

I want to especially thank a master third grade teacher of twenty years, my mother, Susan Trask, for her help with this book. As I considered my own experiences in teaching third grade, collected ideas from colleagues, and worked at shaping them into this book, she was a constant sounding board. I appreciate all of the expertise and time she was willing to share. Thanks, Mom!

Another group of people also deserve acknowledgments for their contributions to this book. The dedicated and inspiring professionals at Northeast Foundation for Children have been guiding child-based teaching and learning for many years, and the influence that they have had on my career can't be measured. Margaret Berry Wilson, Alice Yang, and Michael Lain were especially instrumental in the crafting of this book. I'd also like to thank Helen Merena for sharing her incredible gifts of design. Her work made this book so easy to pick up and enjoy!

Finally, and most importantly, I want to thank my wife, Heather, for helping me stay well-balanced, healthy, and sane, and my two children, Ethan and Carly, for reminding me constantly about why it's so important for American education to be vibrant and inspiring.

 **Mike Anderson** is a *Responsive Classroom*® consultant with Northeast Foundation for Children and has been presenting *Responsive Classroom* workshops since 1999. Mike taught third, fourth, and fifth grades for fifteen years in Connecticut and New Hampshire. In 2004, he was the recipient of a Milken National Educator Award for excellence in teaching.

Mike is the author of two other books in the *What Every Teacher Needs to Know* series (fourth grade and fifth grade), plus *The Well-Balanced Teacher* (ASCD, 2010) and *The Research-Ready Classroom* (with co-author Andy Dousis; Heinemann, 2006). Mike lives in Durham, New Hampshire, with his wife, Heather, and their two children, Ethan and Carly.

About the *Responsive Classroom*® Approach

All of the recommended practices in this book come from or are consistent with the *Responsive Classroom* approach. Developed by classroom teachers and backed by independent research, the *Responsive Classroom* approach emphasizes social, emotional, and academic growth in a strong and safe school community. The goal is to enable optimal student learning. The following are strategies within the *Responsive Classroom* approach, along with resources for learning about each.

All these resources are published by Northeast Foundation for Children and available from WWW.RESPONSIVECLASSROOM.ORG ∎ 800-360-6332.

Morning Meeting: Gathering as a whole class each morning to greet one another, share news, and warm up for the day ahead

111

> *99 Activities and Greetings: Great for Morning Meeting . . . and other meetings, too!* by Melissa Correa-Connolly. 2004.

> *Doing Math in Morning Meeting: 150 Quick Activities That Connect to Your Curriculum* by Andy Dousis and Margaret Berry Wilson with an introduction by Roxann Kriete. 2010.

> *Morning Meeting Activities in a Responsive Classroom* DVD. 2008.

> *The Morning Meeting Book* by Roxann Kriete with contributions by Lynn Bechtel. 2002.

> *Morning Meeting Greetings in a Responsive Classroom* DVD. 2008.

> *Morning Meeting Messages K–6: 180 Sample Charts from Three Classrooms* by Rosalea S. Fisher, Eric Henry, and Deborah Porter. 2006.

> *Sample Morning Meetings in a Responsive Classroom* DVD and viewing guide. 2009.

Foundation-Setting During the First Weeks of School: Taking time during the critical first weeks of school to establish expectations, routines, a sense of community, and a positive classroom tone

> *The First Six Weeks of School* by Paula Denton and Roxann Kriete. 2000.

> *Guided Discovery in a Responsive Classroom* DVD. 2010.

> *Teaching Children to Care: Classroom Management for Ethical and Academic Growth, K–8,* revised ed., by Ruth Sidney Charney. 2002.

Positive Teacher Language: Using words and tone as a tool to promote children's active learning, sense of community, and self-discipline

> *The Power of Our Words: Teacher Language That Helps Children Learn* by Paula Denton, EdD. 2007.

> *Teacher Language in a Responsive Classroom* DVD. 2009.

Rule Creation and Logical Consequences: Helping students create classroom rules to ensure an environment that allows all class members to meet their learning goals; responding to rule-breaking in a way that respects students and restores positive behavior

> *Creating Rules with Students in a Responsive Classroom* DVD. 2007.

> *Rules in School: Teaching Discipline in the Responsive Classroom,* 2nd ed., by Kathryn Brady, Mary Beth Forton, and Deborah Porter. 2011.

Interactive Modeling: Teaching children to notice and internalize expected behaviors through a unique modeling technique

> *Rules in School: Teaching Discipline in the Responsive Classroom,* 2nd ed., by Kathryn Brady, Mary Beth Forton, and Deborah Porter. 2011.

> *Teaching Children to Care: Classroom Management for Ethical and Academic Growth, K–8,* revised ed., by Ruth Sidney Charney. 2002.

Classroom Organization: Setting up the physical room in ways that encourage students' independence, cooperation, and productivity

> *Classroom Spaces That Work* by Marlynn K. Clayton with Mary Beth Forton. 2001.

Movement, Games, Songs, and Chants: Sprinkling quick, lively activities throughout the school day to keep students energized, engaged, and alert

16 Songs Kids Love to Sing performed by Pat and Tex LaMountain. 1998.

99 Activities and Greetings: Great for Morning Meeting . . . and other meetings, too! by Melissa Correa-Connolly. 2004.

Doing Math in Morning Meeting: 150 Quick Activities That Connect to Your Curriculum by Andy Dousis and Margaret Berry Wilson with an introduction by Roxann Kriete. 2010.

Energizers! 88 Quick Movement Activities That Refresh and Refocus, K–6 by Susan Lattanzi Roser. 2009.

Morning Meeting Activities in a Responsive Classroom DVD. 2008.

Solving Behavior Problems With Children: Engaging children in solving their behavior problems so they feel safe, challenged, and invested in changing

Solving Thorny Behavior Problems: How Teachers and Students Can Work Together by Caltha Crowe. 2009.

Sammy and His Behavior Problems: Stories and Strategies from a Teacher's Year by Caltha Crowe. 2010. (Also available as an audiobook.)

Working With Families: Hearing parents' insights and helping them understand the school's teaching approaches

Parents & Teachers Working Together by Carol Davis and Alice Yang. 2005.

About Child Development

Understanding children's development is crucial to teaching them well. To learn more about child development, see the following resources:

Child and Adolescent Development for Educators by Michael Pressley and Christine McCormick. Guilford Press. 2007. This textbook presents understandable explanations of theories and research about child development and suggests ways to apply those theories and research to classroom teaching.

Child Development, 8th ed., by Laura E. Berk. Pearson Education, Inc. 2009. This textbook summarizes the history and current thinking about child development in easy-to-understand prose. The author outlines the major theories and research and provides practical guidance for teachers.

Child Development Guide by the Center for Development of Human Services, SUNY, Buffalo State College. WWW.BSC-CDHS.ORG/FOSTERPARENTTRAINING/PDFS/CHILDDEVELGUIDE.PDF. The center presents characteristics of children at each stage of development in an easy-to-use guide for foster parents.

"The Child in the Elementary School" by Frederick C. Howe in *Child Study Journal*, Vol. 23, Issue 4. 1993. The author presents the common characteristics of students at each grade level, identified by observing students and gathering teacher observations.

"How the Brain Learns: Growth Cycles of Brain and Mind" by Kurt W. Fischer and Samuel P. Rose in *Educational Leadership*, Vol. 56: 3, pp. 56–60. November 1998. The authors, who blend the study of child development with neuroscience, summarize their prior work in a format intended for educators. They conclude that "both behavior and the brain change in repeating patterns that seem to involve common growth cycles."

"The Scientist in the Crib: A Conversation with Andrew Meltzoff" by Marcia D'Arcangelo in *Educational Leadership*, Vol. 58: 3, pp. 8–13. November 2000. Written in an interview format, this article dispels myths about child development and explores ways in which research about cognitive development might inform the work of educators.

Yardsticks: Children in the Classroom Ages 4–14, 3rd ed., by Chip Wood. Northeast Foundation for Children. 2007. This highly practical book for teachers and parents offers narratives and easy-to-scan charts of children's common physical, social-emotional, cognitive, and language characteristics at each age from four through fourteen and notes the classroom implications of these characteristics.

Your Child: Emotional, Behavioral, and Cognitive Development from Birth through Preadolescence by AACAP (American Academy of Child and Adolescent Psychiatry) and David Pruitt. Harper Paperbacks. 2000. Intended for parents, this book presents information about children's development and offers tips for helping children develop appropriately.

ABOUT THE PUBLISHER

Northeast Foundation for Children, Inc., a nonprofit educational organization, is the developer of the *Responsive Classroom®* approach to teaching. We offer the following for elementary school educators:

PUBLICATIONS AND RESOURCES

■ Books, CDs, and DVDs for teachers and school leaders

■ Professional development kits for school-based study

■ Website with extensive library of free articles:
WWW.RESPONSIVECLASSROOM.ORG

■ Free quarterly newsletter for elementary educators

■ The *Responsive®* blog, with news, ideas, and advice from and for elementary educators

PROFESSIONAL DEVELOPMENT SERVICES

■ Introductory one-day workshops for teachers and administrators

■ Week-long institutes offered nationwide each summer and on-site at schools

■ Follow-up workshops and on-site consulting services to support implementation

■ Development of teacher leaders to support schoolwide implementation

■ Resources for site-based study

■ National conference for administrators and teacher leaders

FOR DETAILS, CONTACT:

Responsive Classroom®

Northeast Foundation for Children, Inc.
85 Avenue A, Suite 204, P.O. Box 718
Turners Falls, Massachusetts 01376-0718

800-360-6332 ■ www.responsiveclassroom.org
info@responsiveclassroom.org